The Gambia:
Land of the Mandinka

Susan Rogers

Published by Pip & Tinks Publishing

ISBN: 978-0-9928634-4-9

Other books in the Travelling Solo series

Vietnam: A Journey of Unexpected Delights
Brazil and Argentina: From Jungle to Icebergs

This book is dedicated to Richard and Sarah,
(you know who you are!) for being the most perfect holiday
company.

ACKNOWLEDGMENTS

Thank you Aaron Hendricks (Aaronik Designs) for the front

cover design.

Thanks to my sister, Sally Ann May, for proof reading.

Table of Contents

Introduction

This is the third book in the *"Travelling Solo"* series.

The first, *"Vietnam: Journey of unexpected Delights"* was about a holiday where I thought I was joining a tour group, only to find that group consisted of one person – me! After initial wobbles about having nobody to eat with, talk with and share memories with, accepted my lot and ended up having the most fantastic holiday ever. From that point on, I decided that I wouldn't join formal tour groups again, and instead, indulge in solo travel.

The second book was about my journey to parts of Brazil and Argentina, which was specifically designed as solo travel, and was the most amazing and enjoyable experience, including the Iguaçu Falls, the Amazon jungle and the glaciers of Patagonia. I especially loved the Amazon and to this day it has a special place in my heart.

This third book covers not only a single week in The Gambia in 2012, but reflections and amusing anecdotes from earlier visits.

Day 1 - Getting Away

I didn't sleep a wink, which was probably just as well because the mobile phone alarm didn't go off as planned. I was awake though to turn off the main alarm just before it screeched out. There are times when I need to be up and my natural body clock acts as in internal alarm, but as I needed to be out of bed by 4.30am, my reliance on electronic devices was imperative. At 4.30 am, I had half an hour to take a bath, have a large strong cup of coffee and get my act together before leaving for Gatwick.

The excitement was palpable. Indeed, I was so excited to be going on holiday that I didn't really care that I hadn't had any more than two hours of fitful sleep. I'd taken holidays in recent years, though mainly strenuous back packing trips to Scotland, The Lake District and The Pyrenees, and although beautiful and being exposed to stunning scenery, travelling with a zealous mountain walker had meant that they felt more like route marches and endurance tests than holidays. This holiday was going to be special. It was the first long haul I'd taken in seven and a half years. A combination of running a successful marketing consultancy giving me little time to take a vacation, and being in a relationship with the zealous mountain walker who thought that Switzerland was long haul, had curtailed my distant travels. I was now free of the zealot, business had slowed down as the recession bit harder, and I was treating myself to a single week of rest and relaxation.

I was of course travelling solo, having discovered the joys of such travel during my trip to Vietnam nearly 10 years earlier. I had thought I was joining an organised tour, when I booked the trip to Vietnam, however on arrival in Saigon, discovered that there was only one person in the tour – me. After initial wobbles, I went on to have the most fantastic and memorable holiday, so that when I booked my next trip, to Brazil and Argentina, there was no question that it would be solo travel. Outside an organised tour, you get to see behind the tourist façade, get to meet the real people of the country and dip your toe into their culture in a much more significant way than you could otherwise. With just a few weeks holiday, you can never totally absorb yourself into a foreign world, but you do get those few steps closer when travelling alone.

With the bath completed, suitcase closed and locked and my watch showing 5.07am, seven minutes later than I would have liked, I was still confident that I could make it to Gatwick by 7.00am, on the basis that I anticipated little traffic at that time of the day. The traffic turned out to be incredibly light and I was far too cautious with my contingency time, so I arrived at Gatwick by 6.15am. As I approached the airport, there was a noticeable increase in vehicles moving slowly towards the metropolis, and I thanked my lucky stars that I was no longer a daily commuter into the capital.

Everything ran remarkably smoothly; the parking, the transfer to the airport and spotting the check-in desk. There was a brief shiver when I stepped into the transit bus to be assaulted by sweaty underwear smells, stale beer fumes and the screech of infants, who had clearly learned from a very early age that the more persistently they screamed, the sooner they got the comforter pushed back into their mouth, but overall, nothing was going to dampen my mood.

The Monarch check in desk queue wasn't too long, so I breathed a sigh of relief as I was pretty desperate for the loo, but on balance would rather wait a few more minutes to check in than try and navigate the toilet facilities with both my main suitcase and a small rucksack.

At least half of the people at the check-in were Gambian, or of Gambian descent. I watched with some amusement as a family tried to check in with a ridiculous amount of luggage. They were just mum, dad and one small child. She put her suitcase, the size that murderers use for body disposal, onto the weighing block, and it weighed in at 37 kilos. The limit was only 20 kilos. There were two more suitcases of similar size and weight, along with three pieces of cabin baggage the same size as most people's check-in luggage.

"Only 20 kilos per person," the check in girl explained.

"But what are we to do," replied the large flustered Gambian lady, waving her arms in the long voluminous sleeves, giving the impression that she was about to take to flight.

"I'm sorry," continued the check-in girl, "those are the rules. 20 kilos per person. However, if you would like to pay for additional weight, it is £50 per kilo."

The Gambian lady shook her head. "It is no problem, I will squeeze some more into my hand luggage."

The limit for hand luggage was just five kilos per person, and even a young child mastering the basics of maths would see that the sums just didn't add up. The conversation continued for a further few minutes with the content just going around and around in circles. The family left the desk without checking in, to go and try to pour around 50 kilos of excess weight into hand luggage that was already bursting at the seams. Quart into a pint sprung to mind, except in their case it was closer to a gallon into a pint..... I didn't see them again so will never know whether they managed the impossible, ditched a load of stuff or paid the extortionate excess baggage fee and boarded the aircraft incognito.

"Are you off on holiday?" an elderly chap behind me in the queue asked.

"Yes, just a quick week away for some R&R," I replied.

"I'm going out partly for work and partly for holiday. Gambia is lovely at this time of the year, just before the monsoon, but as it's "out of season" many restaurants will be closed." I asked him about The Clay Oven, the most authentic Indian restaurant outside of India that I'd ever come across.

"Yes, I reckon they will be open, not just because they are so well known, but it's the only decent Indian restaurant in the area."

Although I was booked for half board at Ngala Lodge, I knew that there would be at least one lunchtime trip to The Clay Oven. I first ate there over 20 years previously and had returned on each of two subsequent visits.

I checked in, dashed to the loo and then headed straight through to departures. It was a while since I'd flown from

Gatwick and the toilet facilities were much improved. Security was also new and tighter and with a significantly more efficient conveyor belt system for hand luggage, with larger trays that automatically dropped off the end and returned to the beginning of the queue. As my tray came out of the x-ray box it was diverted onto a new track which meant it was going to be searched. My circular metal powder compact had raised alarm bells because it went through on its edge and instead of being a flat circular object, it showed up as a long thin metallic object, somewhat akin to a bullet. Once security was satisfied that it was indeed the compact that triggered suspicion and that there were no bullets lurking in the corners of my bag, I was through into the departure lounge.

I needed some caffeine and was also a little peckish, so despite my pre-planning objective to watch the pennies on this trip, I already felt the "holiday bugger-it mode" flowing over me like a surfers wave, which effectively meant no scrimping and making appropriate use of credit cards. I chose Cafe Rouge for a civilised sit down breakfast and two large cups of coffee.

I couldn't be bothered to look around the shops as I wasn't going to buy anything anyway, so checked the board and was delighted to see that my gate was already open. I wandered down. There was one elderly lady ahead of me, otherwise the room was empty, as no doubt the majority of passengers were still stalking the not so cheap duty frees. The room gradually filled up and I smiled at the number of Gambians travelling. Mentally I was already there.

Opposite me there was a young black missionary looking

chap in an oversized suit with baggy trousers and an open neck white shirt. For some reason he reminded me of Sammy Davis Junior in a film I couldn't remember the title of. Next to him was a huge black lady sporting a well used straw hat. She was dressed in traditional, vibrantly coloured Gambian clothes. A long red and orange batik grandmuba over her bright yellow malan (underskirt). I didn't think they knew each other but they chatted away in Mandingo. Two young Gambian mothers sauntered in with their babies strapped to their backs with brightly coloured batik scarves. One had her hair in African braids each secured with a gaudy coloured band and I mused as to whether I'd have my hair plaited this holiday, as I had done 25 years earlier.

Whilst waiting in the boarding room, an official approached the elderly English lady who was there before me, and was now sitting opposite me, and asked her to accompany him. She pushed her stuff back into her giant handbag, her hands shaking and her head twitching, the hallmarks of an alcoholic.

"It's because I'm carrying too much money" she whispered to me conspiratorially, and disappeared with the official. She returned about 10 minutes later and proceeded to tell me the story, in a volume far too inappropriate for the subject matter.

"I'm wearing a money belt". She tapped her waist, pursed her lips and nodded her head knowingly.

"I'm carrying too much money. They spotted my money belt at X-ray when I went through security and I expected them to stop me there and then. They usually do"

Usually? She obviously frequently took a lot of money to Gambia, and her conspiratorial manner begged me to say something. I smiled and asked,

"You're not money laundering are you?"

"Oh no dear" she replied, not entirely sure whether I was joking or not, "I have a house out there and I'm going to buy some new furniture on this trip. I get a much better price if I have cash. I also had problems because I had twenty suitcases full of pens and paper for a local school I'm supporting". Twenty suitcases, wow! I usually take a pack of 100 Bic Biros.

I was surprised how easily she was telling everyone within ear shot that she was carrying a shed load of cash, so I couldn't resist,

"Are you worth mugging then?"

"Oh yes my dear," she said with a twinkle, "Most definitely."

We boarded the Monarch aircraft and to my delight, not only did I have an extra legroom seat that I hadn't specifically requested, as the seats had been pre-allocated, but I also had nobody sitting in the other two seats on my row. However my delight was very short lived as in the row immediately behind me was a young, fidgety Gambian woman with a squawking baby. Sadly, the extra legroom and two empty seats did nothing to prevent the journey being seven hours of hell. It should only have been a 6 hours incarceration, however the inevitable passenger hadn't turned up and we were delayed whilst they unloaded his luggage, thereby missing a couple of take-off slots. More annoying than the screaming brat was the total lack of any attempt on the part of the mother to quell the noise. Even with my headphones on, listening to my music as loud as I dare without equally annoying any other passengers, I was unable to filter out the caterwauling. Even though I tried sitting in the other two seats next to me, I was not buffeted by the aircraft but by the selfish woman behind me who wriggled and fidgeted, throughout the entire flight, back massaging me with her feet and knees and not once offering any apologies to the people around her for giving them the flight from hell. I know I have a low noise tolerance level, but I was certain that others would have been as irritated as me. They used to put smokers at the back of the plane to minimise any inconvenience for the non-smokers. Now that smoking on flights is banned they should allocate the anti-social rear seats to anyone carrying a child. Alternatively, a shoot down into the hold would be so much better. Some may argue that although annoying, the noise and fidgeting is not detrimental to health – but it was to mine. After just two hours sleep it was now the equivalent of 4.00pm and my nerves were frayed.

Banjul airport looked new as we taxied in, and I didn't recognise it from my previous visits. I had to laugh though, as the arrival hall was around fifty paces from the aircraft steps, yet there was a bus twenty-five paces away, which we had to alight to take us around the whole perimeter of this small airfield to eventually stop outside the arrival hall. Once inside, I realised that the "new" airport just had a new facade, and the hall was pretty much exactly as I remembered it. Small, crowded, everyone pushing for passport control with only one booth open for "foreigners". Then there was more pushing and shoving at baggage collection, and then nothing short of a skirmish to get out of the baggage hall, as you had to have all your luggage scanned again and there was only one old fashioned X-ray machine in operation. What made this procedure especially farcical was that nobody was watching the x-rayed luggage, so it was all a bit of a pointless exercise. Initially I tried to stay very British and queue as best I could, however it rapidly became clear that it was every man for himself and the local Gambians especially had no qualms in pushing you out of the way to get closer to the x-ray box. I thought, "when in Rome ...", and started being more luggage assertive.

After eventually being bulldozed into the arrival hall, I made my way outside and alighted the coach to take me to Ngala Lodge. I'd been pronouncing it Ne-gala before the holiday, however the guide on board pronounced it Engala, with a nasal N. The wait on the bus seemed interminable as we waited for those caught up in the luggage skirmish, but eventually the last person arrived unscathed and we were off to the hotel, dropping off others en route. The journey took about forty-five minutes.

One thing struck me immediately. It was 15 years since my last visit, and ... nothing had changed. The old shop fronts, the half built houses, the little piles of rubbish that were burned constantly by the road side, the goats tethered looking like they were going nowhere soon, bony cows wandering freely, the children running alongside the bus waving, old men crouched on their haunches moving their African chewing sticks from one side of their mouth to the other just watching the world pass by without saying a word. Skinny, skinny dogs ferreting in rubbish, ladies carrying loads on their heads, teenage girls in their smart school uniforms carrying their small packages of books looking incongruently smart amid the rest of the tableau. Yep, nothing much had changed in fifteen years. We dropped off at the Senegambia Hotel where I stretched my brain to remember it, having stayed there once, yet nothing was familiar. I found out later that there had been a lot of development around that particular area of the town in recent years, so that was possibly fogging my memory.

We arrived at Ngala Lodge, which from the road looked like any other dilapidated building. It was not a typical hotel, more a boutique lodge, so there wasn't a glossy reception area but a small building at the entrance which was effectively the reception and office, the place where you collected and left your keys, could get money changed and so on. There was an open sided thatched meeting area just inside the grounds, where we were given iced fruit juice drinks and told that our rep would be calling in at the hotel the next morning at 10.30 to find out if we wanted to take any of the tours, or just answer any queries or questions. Part of me thought, I'll give it a miss as it's my fourth visit to The Gambia, and I was planning to spend the week chilling, however on the other hand there were a couple of day trips in the brochure I hadn't done before, such as the early-bird bird watching and the safari day trip to Senegal.....

I was shown to my room, or rather suite, and it was stunningly beautiful.

It was everything the web site promised. There was a living area with two sofas, a desk and fridge. The floor was tiled and the walls painted white, however the room was brought to life with colourful modern Gambian art pictures carefully and tastefully placed. The bedroom was huge, with a large four poster bed adorned in mosquito nets. The bathroom had an unusual shaped sink like a canoe, a walk in shower and separate loo room. There was no television in the room, but I had known this before I came, and was something I could easily survive without for a week and was one of the main things that had attracted me to Ngala, along with the fact that no kids under 16 were allowed. Yes, this hotel was certainly a slice of paradise.

Ngala Lodge was an old colonial building that had been lovingly and tastefully turned into a Lodge Hotel. The owner and his family lived there most of the year, only retreating to Europe during the rainy season. Indeed, they retreated halfway through my stay. For the first time in twelve hours, I started to relax.

This was short lived as my mobile phone wouldn't work. I had turned it off for the flight and now it wouldn't turn on. Nor would it charge. Bugger. This sort of summed up my love hate relationship with technology. When you have it and it works, it is great, when things go wrong, despite any protestations that you don't depend on it, it irks. I wasn't a huge mobile phone user anyway, much preferring a laptop as my weapon of choice. Sometimes I felt as if my laptop had to be welded to my right hand, to the extent that I'd been a laptop traveller for around 15 years.

I recalled a radio four programme about how you can spot a seasoned (business) traveller versus those travelling for the first time. The novice traveller, travels in his business suit and tie, wearing them as a badge to the world to prove he's "made it" to the heights of international business traveller. Result? They arrive crumpled and dishevelled and look like they've slept in the suit for at least 3 days. The seasoned traveller is casual. Perhaps chinos and a loose old sweatshirt or fleece with trainers or loafers. Their business attire is neatly packed in the suitcase, so that when they change at the other end, they are wearing crisp, freshly laundered clothes and exude "I'm ready for serious business".

The novice is so overwhelmed by the array of entertainment options open to him, he spends the entire flight eating, drinking, watching movies and playing hand held games. He may doze off for an hour or two if the flight is a long one to Asia or South America, but if you hadn't spotted him by his crumpled suit, then the crunched up face and bloodshot eyes as you alight will be a giveaway. The seasoned traveller opts for the light menu choice to be served after take-off, with one glass of wine and a bottle of water, then hunkers down to get some essential sleep.

Finally the novice arrives in his opulent five-star international business hotel room, and is wowed by the well stocked mini bar temptingly glittering at him. He also revels in the amazing choice of global channels on the satellite TV, and the library of in-house, on demand films available, that even Blockbuster would be envious of. Not so the seasoned traveller. His first action is to open his briefcase and look for a computer socket. (Bear in mind that these were the days before Wi-Fi). If it meant crawling around under the desk for the second telephone socket and unravelling the spaghetti of wires festooned around the legs of the table, then that's what it took. Only once the internet connection has been established will the seasoned traveller relax, take a shower and get ready for his first business meeting. I had been a seasoned traveller for years. Even on holiday. Indeed I remember one vacation in Greece where their phone socket didn't fit my computer, so using my tweezers as a screwdriver, I took the connection off the hotel phone and fitted it to the end of my lead, so that at least I could pick up email. Sad I know, but hey, that's what I do.

Oh joy! Ngala lodge had Wi-Fi, so even though I didn't have an operational mobile phone, I should at least get internet access for the small laptop. I readied myself for the Wi-Fi to only work in certain areas of the grounds, meaning I'd have to traipse around trying to get a signal, but no, I got a good strong signal right in my room. I started to relax again, although I did spend half an hour surfing the android help forums to see if there was an easy fix for my phone, only to realise that the chances were that it was a frazzled battery, which realistically meant I wasn't going to get it sorted until I returned home. I did however order a new battery on Amazon so that it would be waiting for me.

I turned my attention to unpacking, and suddenly realised that I was excruciatingly tired and still somewhat stressed by the uncomfortable flight, and I wanted a cigarette. I'd packed in smoking 12 months previously, yet at that moment, I felt like I really needed one. I was so tired that I didn't even try and talk myself out of it. Leaving the unpacking, I went down to the reception lodge and asked where I could buy cigarettes.

"No problem madam. We can send someone out for you. What would you like?

"A packet of red Marlboro please."

"How many?"

"Just the one please, oh and a lighter or packet of matches please."

"Certainly madam, but they are not cheap near this hotel. They are 50 Dalasi a packet." My brain wasn't so tired as to be unable to do the calculation. 50 Dalasi was the equivalent of around 70 pence. Back home I believed they were in excess of £7 a packet. I gave him a hundred Dalasi note and told him to keep the change on his return.

I wasn't sure whether I enjoyed the cigarette or not. I liked the taste and the "hit", but it scorched my throat and I felt a little sick after it. However, it served its purpose and relaxed me even more.

I went for a walk around the lodge grounds. It had beautiful, well maintained gardens and most importantly was quiet and peaceful.

It was around thirty-four degrees and extremely humid. Not many people go to Gambia at that time of the year, June, as it's just before the rainy season and humidity is at its highest.

There were beautiful doves flying around. Their collared doves were darker than ours, and there was one with amazing red eyes giving it a rather demonic look.

When I visited The Gambia twenty-five years earlier, I was somewhat scornful of the bird watchers during a boat trip, who orgasmed every time they saw a White Egret, and I could still hear calls of, "Oh look! Another White Egret," as everyone turned their binoculars to the direction of the cry. My ex husband and I had rolled our eyes more than once. However in the past five years, whilst building a nature reserve on my seven acre field along with visiting some commercial nature reserves, I'd become much more interested in our feathered friends, and I smiled to myself as I thought "I hope I see a White Egret". That was why I was interested in the early morning bird tour.

It was now 7.00pm and already getting dark. Dinner was served from 7.30pm, so I had a most welcome shower, dressed and went down to the restaurant, choosing to sit outside on the terrace where there was a gently cooling breeze. There were very few customers, clearly an indication that we were indeed at the end of the tourist season.

The food and service were excellent. I opted for the specials of the day which were a Caesar salad starter followed by lamb with roast vegetables. During the meal I started to write my diary of the trip so far, then carried on reading Jamaica Inn, whilst downing three bottles of Julbrew beer. By 9.00pm I was mellow, full, very tired and ready for bed. The fact that it was pitch black by 8.00pm also gave the illusion that it was closer to midnight.

I set the air conditioning on the coolest setting, turned on the very efficient, high powered pedestal fan, dropped the mosquito nets which were held by delicate bands, crawled under the sheet and immediately fall asleep. I awoke around 4.00am after a nightmare about Fred's caravan next door to me back home.

Another saga for another day, but in brief, I lived in a

farmhouse with no neighbours. Next door was a non-working farm yard with the barns converted into workshops by the son of the person I'd bought my house from. The workshops were rented out to local craftsman, builders and the like, mainly for storage. A month previously, he'd moved in Fred with a small caravan, allegedly to be the night watchman. Fred was scum. A thirty something drop out who wore his one and only camo outfit. He did jobbing work during the day and got drunk and took drugs during the evening, returning late, loud and obnoxious, ruining the peace I'd paid a lot of money for. I had complained to the owner, however he had no balls whatsoever and didn't dare move Fred out in case there were reprisals. The owner also avoided confrontation like the plague. It was causing me untold stress, and apart from the late night noise, he was living there illegally and showed no respect or regard to an honest taxpaying resident next door. I hated him. Before I came away I'd found a pile of human poo at my gate, and when I asked Charlie, the owner, to check his CCTV he'd said "I'm not going to waste time on something so petty". I didn't consider poo being left by my gate as being petty. Yes, I could have kicked up a stink, had Fred evicted, and got Charlie fined, however my house was on the market and I didn't want to cause too many waves before I left the area. This was what the nightmare had been about. It had woken me and I realised that I was having a mild panic attack, with chest palpitations and a sweaty brow. I couldn't get back to sleep, so paced the room for a while and boiled up a mug of decaf coffee. Eventually the memory of the vivid dream left me, so I had a second cigarette and went back to bed.

Day 2 - Exploration

Overall I felt that I'd slept pretty well, despite the nightmare. I slept very badly at home. Had done for years. Then suddenly I knew how I was going to deal with the Fred situation when I got home. Ok, it was a revenge strategy, but I suddenly felt a lot better knowing that I'd have the last word, with no repercussions. With this, I pushed him out of my mind and he didn't re-enter during the week.

It was 7.00am and breakfast was served at 7.30, so sufficient time to shower, get dressed and then venture out. Breakfast was delicious. Fresh fruits (melon and mango), bread and jam, Danish pastries and a Spanish omelette, which was basically an omelette with carrots. I also tried a glass of Baobab juice, which although not totally unpleasant, was probably an acquired taste and not one I wished to acquire, so planned to stick to more familiar juices for the rest of the week.

After breakfast, sitting on my balcony and continuing to read for an hour, I recalled my afternoon cream tea at the very same Jamaica Inn I was reading about, only a matter of weeks previously. The storyline was slightly ruined as when walking in to the lovely Bodmin Moor Inn, I'd spied a plaque saying "On this spot Joss Merlyn was murdered". I hadn't reached Joss' death in the book, so that would be one less surprise, however it didn't mar my overall enjoyment of the story.

With White Egrets calling and an adventure in Senegal beckoning, I decided to attend the welcome meeting after all and moseyed on down to the open reception area. There were only two other couples and myself. Babou J was a smartly dressed professional Gambian around mid forties. He gave us some information about the locality and what we'd find within walking distance. I only half listened as I'd heard most of it before. He explained about being pestered by locals, but emphasised that we were definitely safe. Really I thought, as I cast my mind back to my first visit when Annie and Dick, a couple we'd befriended had been robbed outside of the hotel walls at night. Babou J also mentioned a few scams that had been running that year. One was for a man to approach you saying he is a gardener at your hotel, that he recognised you and would be delighted to give you a guided tour as it was his day off. It would be perfectly safe to go with him, however he didn't work at the hotel, nor was he a guide, but he would expect a few hundred Dalasi as a thank you for his guiding services. The other scam was to be approached by a well dressed man carrying some files and folders. He looked official. He would say that he was a teacher and he'd like to show you some pictures of his school because he was so proud about the developing education system and their school was already half built. Of course he wasn't a school teacher, he didn't even work at a school, and the pictures were taken at a school he had visited also under false pretences. Again, you would have been perfectly safe with this man, however he'd have pressed you for a donation to help them finish building the school, buy school books, stationery or desks and so on.

I was really at the meeting just to book a couple of tours. Yes, I knew my plan was not to do any tours this holiday, however I had already seen some lovely colourful birds in the garden of the hotel and I just had to sign up for the early birds one. 5.30am pick up the following Monday, the day before I returned. I also decided to do the one-day safari trip into Senegal as I hadn't been over the border before.

The first time I visited Gambia was with my ex husband. We'd been about to exchange contracts on our house after an especially long time on the market, and it had all fallen through. We'd both been saving our holiday leave to spend time settling into the new house, so we just decided to escape for a 3 weeks trip to Gambia, and had had a fantastic time, combining relaxation with trips, tours and experiences. The second time I visited had been by myself. I'd had a run of awful things happening within a relatively short period, a shoulder operation, being burgled and then a very good friend dying suddenly. It had been December and as the weather is fantastic in Gambia at that time of the year, I had effectively jumped on a plane to spend some time in the sun just chilling and reflecting on the meaning of life and the universe. The third time had been with a boyfriend. I'd repeated some of the tours for his benefit, but it had mainly been a week of rest and relaxation.

I had two very vivid memories of trips I took the first time in Gambia. One was for an evening meal at Lamin Lodge, and the other was a 2 days trip to Janjanbureh Camp.

Lamin Lodge was a traditional Gambian restaurant, built out of wood with a straw roof and wooden stilts. The food had been a traditional Gambian feast, and the elderly lady who owned or ran it had us all up doing traditional Gambian dancing after the meal. Considering the amount of jumping around and stamping of feet, I was amazed that the hut didn't collapse on it's rickety stilts.

Janjanbureh Camp is on Janjanbureh island, locally called McCarthy Island and where you'll also find Georgetown, again, sometimes called Janjanbureh. Georgetown was founded by the British in the early 1800's and was a thriving and busy trading centre in West Africa. The Camp was a different experience altogether. We travelled for around 5 hours by dirt track in the most uncomfortable Landrover, so that our knees were up by our chins, and our bottoms sore from the combination of hard seats and driving over a cratered track. Eventually we had arrived at a river crossing which had been fascinating in itself as the passengers were expected to help pull the boat across using the wires strung across the river.

We were taken for a brief walk around Georgetown, now a sleepy little village, and shown some old colonial buildings, which were alleged to have been the old slave prisons, however research before the holiday indicated that they were actually warehouses built after the slave trade ceased. However, the fist visit in the 1980's was not long after the televised series of Roots, which is now deemed to be a work of fiction, but at the time was thought to be based on Alex Haley's old ancestors, and that he himself was a descent of Kunte Kinte, a Mandinka boy enslaved, so Georgetown was infamously etched on your brain as a slave trading center. There was even an old lady sitting outside her crumbling mud hut, claiming to be the last surviving descendent of the fictional Kunte Kinte, and for a few Dalasi, you could look inside her hut. We passed on that.

Prior to the holiday I had thought that the Mandinka, (also known as Mandingo, Malinke and Mandinko) were just native to The Gambia, however I discovered that they were a huge

Western African tribe, also found in Guinea, Mali, Sierra Leone, Ivory Coast, Senegal, Burkina Faso, Liberia, Guinea-Bissau, Niger and Mauritania. Although they were widespread in Africa, it's only within The Gambia where they are the largest ethnic group, which was probably why I specifically associated them with that country.

There wasn't really an awful lot to see in Georgtown, and the locals were clearly trying to cash in on their recent saliency because of Roots, so we quickly continued with the journey.

We then climbed into a small rickety boat which took us further up river to Janjanbureh Camp. We'd chosen this experience as it was as close an experience you could have as to what it was like living in a traditional Gambian village. There was no electricity nor running water. We were shown to our traditional round mud hut, with a pointy thatched roof. There was a concrete plinth with a thin straw mattress and one sheet that was to be our bed and a very basic toilet and cracked wash basin. There was a small wooden door and one tiny window covered in a broken mosquito net. There was a large toad hopping across the floor.

"Please get that toad out of here," I implored, "I really don't like them." The ex took off his trainer, scooped it up and placed it back in the jungle. I sat down on the bed and realized that it was indeed concrete and the mattress was wafer thin. A lizard suddenly darted from underneath the bedding and ran up the wall,

"And you are going to have to get that also!" I added. "Indeed, I'm going to wait outside until you've caught it and put it back in the jungle." Ten minutes later the ex called to me,

"Done. No more lizards in the room."

"Where is it then?"

"I caught it in my hands and threw it back into the jungle." I knew he was lying and he knew that I knew he was lying, but for the remainder of the stay we both pretended that there were no more lizards in the hut. It was starting to get dark and we'd been told that dinner would be served on the thatched terrace in the center of the camp, and so we picked our way along the stone path, with just a kerosene lamp to guide us, the noises of croaking creatures and cicadas around us and the rustling of the palms of surrounding trees. It was very dark on the terrace, with only a few kerosene lamps on the buffet table, and none on the eating tables, as guests were expected to use the kerosene lamps they'd been given. We joined a table, ordered some beers from the waiter and headed over to the buffet table.

On a first glance it looked extremely tasty and appetizing. Dishes of rice, platters of salad, roasted sweet potatoes, and several different tureens of meat stews. I was starving, so picked up a plate to start serving myself.

"Wait. Look!" said the ex. "All the food is moving." It wasn't of course, but because of the numerous bugs, beetles and flies crawling over the food, it had the impression that all the food was shimmering on the table.

"I won't be able to eat any of that," he said. "Remember how ill I was in Turkey, and that food didn't have creepy crawlies swarming all over it."

"Just pick them out," I replied, as I heaped food onto my plate. Nothing puts me off food, and if I needed to pick out bugs before I ate it, then I would.

Back at the table, I had to admit that my plate of food did contain an extraordinary number of living creatures, and I probably ate some I hadn't seen, but I diligently picked out the bugs and flies, and ate dinner. The ex ate nothing. Probably as disconcerting as the bugs, were the locusts. They were attracted to the light from the lamps, and throughout the meal we were constantly bombarded by them as they hit our limbs when leaping to be near the light. My scalp felt incredibly itchy from the heat of the day and thoughts about the bugs around us. Deciding that the only way to survive the evening was to knock myself out, I drank several beers, which were not refreshing as they were all warm.

There were some dancers after dinner, demonstrating trial dancing, but it wasn't as good nor as professional as in Lamin Lodge, so we retreated early to our bed. The heat inside the hut was suffocating. With only one very tiny window and a totally still night there was no air circulation. I doubt either of us had much sleep, and of course at the back of my mind was the knowledge that there was still a lizard in there. We survived the heat of the night by ironically sweating. The single sheet, became damp very quickly, and then when that cooled down, it was actually quite pleasant having the damp cloth against our skins. But then it would get hot again, we'd sweat more, the cloth would dampen and then we'd cool, and so we passed the night in this manner.

The first thing that went though my mind when I awoke was, "I can't believe it – we survived!" Desperate for a wash, I made my way to the shower cubicles that had been pointed out on our arrival. These were canvas tents with an open top, with a bucket hanging over your head, a piece of rope attached to it to tip it over you. The bucket was filled from the river Gambia, so was cold, and very very brown. I didn't mind the cold water as that was a relief, however I think it's the only time I've taken shower and stepped out dirtier than when I stepped in.

There was a short jungle walk to point out some of the flora to us, and then it was retracing our steps from the previous day, with another long and uncomfortable Landrover drive back to Banjul. We were staying at the Atlantic Hotel, which at the time was one of the best hotels in Gambia, and although having a high star rating was somewhat in need of a lick of paint and a general facelift. On arrival we'd thought it was closer to a two star than a four start hotel, however when we returned from Janjanbureh Camp, hot, aching and tired, and the extremely hungry ex, the Atlantic Hotel looked and felt like a palace and we'd have both given it six stars if we'd had to rate it that evening.

Neither of us had enjoyed that trip, even though it had certainly been an experience, and were glad that although it felt like we'd been away a week, it was only two days, and an experience we both swore we'd never repeat.

So as, Babou J rattled through the tours on offer, it sent a shiver down my back when he mentioned Janjanbureh Camp.

He also explained the tipping procedure at the hotel. We

were asked not to tip individuals during the week but to prepare 3 envelopes at the end of our stay. One would be for housekeeping, the second for the kitchen staff and the third for general services, which included people like the guards and grounds men. Tips were shared out so that everyone benefitted, and so that it wasn't down to luck if one waitress had an exceptionally generous tipper whereas another for identical services ended up serving Scrooge. It was also advantageous to the staff you rarely came in contact with, such as the gardeners, who performed an excellent service to keep the hotel looking so stunning, yet were rarely tipped directly. I guessed that this would also mean that all the staff would be courteous and attentive during your stay, not just in the anticipation of a good tip, but it would mean that colleagues would look out for the behaviour of others to ensure that tips were not reduced by poor service and their share forfeited.

With the two tours booked, I made enquiries as to where I could have my hair braided into African plaits, and I was told to speak to Jasmine in the restaurant as she'd be able to sort it for me with her contacts. After the meeting finished, I searched out Jasmine and asked her about hair plaiting. She said that she would mention it to a friend of hers, who would come over to meet me, examine my hair and then give me a price.

It was time to go out and have an adventure. I planned to walk to Cape Point about three miles away, have a drink, possibly lunch and then walk back again. The whole outing looked like it should last around 3 hours, so there would be time in the afternoon to chill in the sun and read or snooze.

I left the guarded gates of the hotel, stepped out onto the dusty, sandy road, and was immediately verbally assaulted with calls of "Taxi! Taxi!" from various drivers. I shook my head, smiled pleasantly, a genuine smile whilst moving my fingers like little puppets saying,

"No thanks, I'm off for a walk".

Within a few yards from the hotel four children come running up to me shouting "Hello! Hello!". Again I smiled and said hello, but kept walking. One of them was carrying what initially looked like a dead cat by its tail, but it wasn't. I moved a little closer out of curiosity, only to realise that it was a dead rat, the size of a cat. The child was gripping the tail tightly and swaying the rat from side to side. I wriggled my nose and said "Ugh, no", shaking my head to ensure they understood what was I was saying. Of course children, being children, they instantly realised that I didn't like the rat, so came running after me swinging it harder and giggling. I walked faster. So did they. I crossed the road. So did they. I eventually walked up to an ATM and pretended to be reading the signs, although I was watching the kids' reflections through the glass window. They eventually got bored and wandered off. Phew. That rat deserved to be in the Guinness Book of Records for it's size.

There were not many buildings during the first part of the walk, just some gardens and a football pitch. There was a lot of rubbish lying around even though the air was pungent with the smell of burning rubbish from yesterday. There were little smouldering bonfires along the side of the road. I passed a few small groups of men sitting around doing nothing, and they all shouted,

"Hello! How are you!" as I passed, and I replied whist still walking,

"Hello. Fine thank you." I could hear the pounding of disco music and realised that I was about to pass the army barracks. There were a couple of mini tanks parked outside the entrance, freshly painted in sort of camo colours, but the greens were brighter than one would expect, bordering on day-glow. Considering that the overall colour scheme of Gambia is sandy browns, and dull olive greens, if these tanks were in action there would be no way they would be "camouflaged". Several soldiers were casually hanging around outside the wall. Nobody appeared to actually be on duty, unless these casual guys were it. I passed the entrance which gave me a good view of the brightly coloured bungalow accommodation, which frankly looked more like a Butlins holiday camp than the army headquarters. This was where the disco music was coming from. The soldiers all shouted variations of,

"Hello! How are you? Which country?". I smiled, waved and continued walking, but added,

"What's happening in there? It sounds like you are having a party?"

"We are always partying," came the reply, "You wanna come in?" I laughed, flicked my hand, my finger moving from side to side giving the internationally known sign of no thanks, and carried on. I was then approaching a row of shack type shops, their frontages open straight onto the dusty street. I'd like to have had a browse as they were mainly craft shops and batik stalls, however I knew that even half a glance at anything would mean that I'd be drawn into an interminable conversation of "Hello! Where you from? Which country? When you get here? When you leave? Come and see my lovely things". I really didn't want to be drawn into discussing why I didn't actually need six carved wooden Mandinka warrior statues at a "good price".

It was then I picked up my first shadow. A young chap in his late twenties.

"Hello! My name is Suma. What is yours?"

I hesitated for a moment, as memories of my first trip to India flashed though my mind. That had been an organised tour and the guide had warned us that there would be a lot of beggars asking for money or sweets, or pressing scraps of paper into our hands with their address written on, hoping for a donation when we returned home. She's said,

"Once you start a conversation it will be very difficult to extricate yourselves. Even saying "no", is starting a conversation. The best thing to do is ignore them, look straight ahead and carry on walking. You will see some very distressing things such as deformed beggars, lepers and tiny dirty children, and I have no doubt that your hearts will go out to all of them, however, please remember, that if you give some money to any of them, they are unlikely to benefit, as their pimp will be lurking nearby to rapidly take their "earnings". If you want to help, there are two ways I would recommend. Firstly, put some money into their economy by buying little trinkets and post cards from the stalls. Even if you bin the trinkets when you return to the hotel, you will have put some money into the economy. The second way is to consider sponsoring a child through one of the well known international aid companies when you return home." I had bought some trinkets which ended in the bin, and I did sponsor two Indian children when back in the UK. But this wasn't India, and the streets were relatively quiet, and with walking out alone, I didn't want to create any hassle, so decided that the most appropriate action would be to appear polite, but carry on walking with a purpose.

"Susan," I replied monosyllabically and continued along the road. He thrust his palm out and said,

"Hello Susan. Welcome to Gambia".

He was scruffy, not quite rags, but scruffy dirty clothes. He had crooked rotten teeth and a sardonic smile. Although I carried on walking, I was shadowed for about half a mile as he kept the conversation flowing. He wanted to know the usual stuff. When did I arrive, when was I going, was it the first visit to The Gambia, which hotel was I staying in, did I need a guide, and so on. My smile became less genuine and more fixed, my walking pace speeded up and my answers were more clipped and abrupt. He was like an annoying piece of goose grass that I just couldn't shake off. I saw the fishing port to my right so crossed the road to go and have a closer look. As I turned into the side street leading to the fishing quay I was aware that the shadow was still with me. He started telling me the names of the boats, which of course I could read for myself and any interest in going further down to the quay oozed away. I headed back to the main road and the shadow followed me.

"You like football? I like football. Manchester United. Yes, I like Manchester United."

I didn't answer him so he carried on,

"What do you like?"

"Gardening" was my response, hoping that this would be a subject of which he couldn't follow, but no, he quickly said,

"My mother likes gardening".

Arghh! I then passed a dirty smelly alleyway leading towards a shanty area. There were tumbledown shacks and shops. It was their local food market. Shadow piped up,

"This is Bakau market. You want me to show you around?" Even though it was especially smelly with rotting veg and meat, and spurious looking liquids creating rivulets in the mud, I'd normally have liked to have had a poke around or at least a walk through, but it was very hot and humid and as it was approaching midday and I just wanted to shake off my shadow, who had started patting my arm with every sentence he uttered.

"No, I don't want to see the market, and actually, I'd like to continue alone please."

I give him the biggest false smile I could muster, turned away from him and walked off. I saw out of the corner of my eye that he made a few half hearted steps to follow, then broke off, turned around and headed away in the opposite direction.

I passed another row of shack shops selling material products and crafts. I needed a long pair of trousers for my early bird watching in case there were a lot of mozzies around on the water, so I ventured into a shack with three ladies squatting on the floor chatting amiably. They showed me three pairs of simple cotton trousers and I selected the blue ones, not just because blue is my favourite colour, but their subdued pattern would be less conspicuous back in the UK. We started the inevitable bargaining at four hundred and fifty Dalasi, which was about £9.50. I started at 150 Dalasi, and after both sides have gone through several rounds of the obligatory "no, you must be joking tactics" we settled at two hundred and seventy five.

After the shops come the various country embassy buildings with some residential mansions slotted in-between. There were very few people around so I carried on with my walk unimpeded. I knew that the Sunset Beach Hotel was at Cape Point, so that was where I'd stop for a long cold beer and a bite to eat.

Just when I was feeling safe and solo, and stopped to take a photo of a vulture flying overhead, I picked up Velcro Man, who had an alarming physical similarity to scumbag Fred, expect of course he was a black Gambian, and was also missing half his teeth. I went through pretty much the same conversation I had had with Shadow, although this time I was more monosyllabic from the beginning. Although we'd been told it was safe to go out, and these people meant no harm, they were just out to make a quick buck from tourists when they could, I was still on guard all of the time when out and about in foreign countries, especially since I was mugged in Budapest when there on business about 10 years previously. We passed within spitting distance of the crocodile park. Whether the Gambians believe the myth, or know that it's just created for the tourists, they say that if you touch a crocodile it will bring you good luck, especially if you are trying to conceive. Well as I was way past that, and had actually seen the crocs on an earlier trip, I now just wanted to get to Sunset Beach. Velcro Man was significantly more persistent than Shadow though, and was really keen to take me to see the crocs.

"I can take you to see Charlie. He is very old croc. Very famous." Charlie was their star act, and I had a photo of me stroking Charlie 15 years previously. Could it be the same Charlie? Possibly? Did I want to find out?...no...not especially.....

I reached the hotel with Velcro Man still gabbling away in my ear. I occasionally nodded, but said very little. Velcro Man then told me that Sunset Beach was closed for the season. I already knew that a lot of hotels would be closed because there were so few tourists, and indeed at Ngala there was only myself and four other couples, however Babou J had led us to believe that the one at Cape Point was open. Perhaps there was another? As if he could read my mind, Velcro Man interjected,

"There is a restaurant on the beach. You can get food and drink there." And guess what, he said that he be able to take me there.

"You can have a drink and then I can take you to see the crocodiles. You can stroke Charlie." As I must had said at least a dozen times that I didn't want to see Charlie, I ignored him and carried on walking down the slipway to the beach. Even my plastic smile had disappeared. My plan was to reach the beach restaurant, have a drink and some lunch and then get the proprietor to call me a taxi back to Ngala. I was in a pretty desolated area. Having recently read Kapka Kassabova's book Villa Pacifica, I suddenly thought of Villa Pacifica being like Ngala in its hay day, and then like this abandoned beach with a few empty shacks dotted around, during the downturn.

It was a large, wide, curving beach, edged with high elephant grass. There were one or two locals walking by the sea edge, but absolutely no buildings in sight whatsoever. I was on the defensive with my right hand clenched in a Taekwondo curl ready to strike if needed be. I'd never had to use it in the 30 years since I learned how to at University, but my senses were on full alert, and I was ready, and in no doubt, that despite being very rusty, this one particular punch would give me sufficient time to escape. Velcro Man commented on the number of scars on my arms and asked if they were mosquito bites. I just shook my head, and carried on walking. They were not, but I had no desire to explain to him that having spent years chopping back spiky hawthorn bushes, and also having rock climbing accidents as well as being generally accident prone, my arms did look at if I'd done a few rounds with a Samurai. He wouldn't understand, but he ran a few paces to catch me up and patted me on the arm. He repulsed me and I created distance between the two of us without making him aware that I was on full alert.

"Where is this restaurant?"

I couldn't see anything even resembling a picnic table.

"Just around the corner" he replied "If it wasn't for the long grass you'd be able to see it now."

I hated walking in sand unless it was hard and compact. It felt like I was dragging my feet through a dusty quagmire. Sand gets everywhere. In your socks, shoes and then somehow manages to migrate all over the hotel room and into the locked suitcase in the corner. You find grains of it years later. Why people choose beach holidays to be submerged in grit not only for the fortnight, but for the next 3 months back home, never ceased to amaze me.

The sand was soft and deep under my trainers and each step felt heavier and heavier as we plodded forward. Velcro Man kept on chatting but I filtered out most of it. We passed some empty colourful wooden juice stalls standing proudly in a row. In the main tourist season the beach would be crowded and there would be queues wanting to buy a chilled juice, but now it looked like a scene from On the Beach.

We eventually turned the corner. There was an empty restaurant with upturned chairs on the tables.

"Is this it?" I said with exasperation "It looks pretty damned closed to me!"

"No, no, further round," he gesticulated.

We rounded the corner a little further, saw a shack a few hundred yards ahead, and Velcro Man was delighted that we had found it. It was deserted. The fridge in the corner was empty and switched off.

"I guess this is closed as well!" I sighed.

"No, no, I will find the man. We will have a drink and then

we'll go and see the crocodiles." Although his English was very good, Velcro Man clearly did not appear to understand "I DO NOT WANT TO GO AND SEE THE CROCODILES!!!!!". He banged on the barren counter and shouted a few sentences in Mandinka. After a few minutes and several repetitions of "can't you see it is closed" from me, a man emerged from the back of the shack. I asked him if it was a restaurant, and he replied only in the tourist season, but he could get me a bottle of Coca-Cola, mumbling that it hadn't been refrigerated.

I was thirsty and starting to get the wobblies from not eating, yet said,

"No thanks, I want a restaurant." What I didn't say was, "the last thing I want is a sickly warm bottle of Coca-Cola!" He pointed towards a group of buildings in the distance, civilisation, and I set off towards them. I was feeling more comfortable now that we are heading back towards habitation, but I didn't drop my guard. Velcro Man was of course only two steps behind me. We reached the buildings having not spoken a word for ten minutes. The streets were nothing more than sandy dirt tracks but the buildings oozed opulence. This was definitely the posh area of Banjul. We arrived at the gates of the Italian restaurant that both Velcro Man and Shack Man had assured me would be open, and it was closed. Velcro Man banged on the door and shouted, but clearly there was nobody inside. I now just wanted to find a taxi to take me back to the hotel. It was hot, very hot and I was in definite need of food.

"But you haven't seen the crocodiles yet," he whinged.

"I want to go back to the hotel. I need some lunch and I'm not going to wander the street of Cape Point hoping that a miracle will happen and we stumble across an open restaurant or hotel. Where can I find the nearest taxi please?" He had eventually got the message. There was no mention of crocodiles and he said that he would call a friend who had a taxi.

"Is he a real taxi driver," I asked, not entirely convinced "Does he drive a yellow and black cab?"

"Yes. Yellow taxi," came the reply. He phoned the friend and passed the phone to me to say hello and to prove to his friend that there was indeed a real customer waiting. With the phone put away, he suggested that we wait down an alley way. Why on earth would anyone want to wait down an alley when it's almost certain that the taxi would approach on the main road, so I just said,

"I'm waiting here."

There were vultures flying around and I wanted to get some good shots, but I was reluctant to divert my attention from Velcro Man, so I let them fly around above me, unphotographed. After ten minutes I said,

"Where is your friend?"

"He's coming he's coming! I'll call him again."

At that moment a yellow taxi appeared around the corner and I sighed with relief.

"Here he is!"

"No, no! That is not my friend."

The taxi pulled over, I opened the door and said to the smiling, genuinely smiling face inside "Ngala Lodge please."

Velcro man strode over still shouting,

"No, this is not my friend. You have to wait for my friend."

Seated inside I tried to close the door, but Velcro Man was hanging on like a limpet.

"We must wait for my friend." I told the driver to drive off and as he moved forward, Velcro Man released his grasp and I closed the door to a torrent of vocabulary, which I can only assume to be Gambian verbal abuse. I thanked the driver and explained that Velcro man had become a little too persistent.

He was probably an okay chap, just trying to earn a few Dalasi for being what he thought as a useful guide. However, we live in an increasingly awful world where people disappear without a trace, so I wasn't going to give him the benefit of the doubt.

Back at the hotel I shed my sand filled trainers for flip flops and headed down to the restaurant for beer and a lunch. Jasmine approached me.

"Excuse me. I have seen my friend who does hair. She will come by this afternoon to look at your hair."

"Great. Thanks for organising that Jasmine, I'll be reading in the garden over there," and pointed to a sunbed. After lunch, and an extra beer to chill from the mornings adventure I strolled over to the sun lounger in the beautiful gardens. The porter appeared from nowhere and brought me a mattress and towel, and I settled down to read my book.

It was hot. Very hot. Very humid. Very sticky, and with the lunchtime beers I started to dose off.

I awoke with a start when Jasmine arrived with Ay-ya who hardly spoke any English, but who combed her fingers through my hair and said something to Jasmine. Jasmine translated,

"It will cost 800 Dalasi to plait your hair, however as it is very fine, not as thick and wiry like African hair it won't stay in place very long so she will need to get some extensions."

I agreed to go ahead with the hairdressing appointment and after a further exchange of Mandinka, Jasmine informed me that Ay-ya would come to my room at 8.00am the next day so that she could finish by 3.00pm. Seven hours to have my hair plaited? I decided at that point to have wider plaits to reduce the time.

I could only cope with an hour of the heat humidity combo, so retired to my room, set my stall out on the balcony along with the large electric upright fan, and continued reading my book in comfort. I finished the book, and although I thoroughly enjoyed it, decided that once the suspense had been revealed, you could never forget how it ended, so it would be a book to be left in the room at the end of the week.

Time on holiday becomes warped. It can feel like only an hour or two have passed, but as it started to darken outside I realised it was time to shower, dress and go down to dinner. There were four outside tables, the remainder being in the restaurant. The other couples had taken the three tables set for two people, so as I wished to eat outside I sit at the remaining one, set for four.

Peter, the owner, a Dutch guy who'd pass as the spitting image for the actor Trevor Howard, came over and asked if I was enjoying my stay and if the room was fine. Yes, everything was fine, it was a beautiful hotel. There were two other guests that I haven't mentioned before, probably because I didn't want to waste ink on them, but they must now be woven into the story.

They were an English couple, both in their late sixties / early seventies and both spoke with Oxford English accents. They were also exceedingly loud. I knew their politics, because everyone could hear their conversation, and I also knew that they read The Telegraph as he was quoting stories of the day to her. She had been here a week and he arrived on the same flight as me. I heard him bragging to his wife that he got a free lift to the hotel on the same transfer bus I used. His name wasn't on a list because he hadn't booked transfers, but went along the row of buses, saw the one with an Ngala Lodge sticker in the front and got on, claiming to the poor Gambian desperately seeking his name on the list, that the list had to have been wrong. He blamed The Gambia Experience tour operator for letting him down. I remembered then, the loud, overbearing and bombastic man at the front of the coach. It had been too hot to argue, so the bus driver had let him on.

She looked well travelled. Thin, with good posture and brown weathered skin like a favourite leather handbag that you can't bear to discard. She had that look of having been on many adventure type long haul holidays, though probably did it all first class. Possibly a memsahib in India at some point.

He was shorter than her, by a few inches, and was fat. He looked like the business type who had spent too many years dining out rather than actually doing any work. He was balding with wispy sandy white hair across his crown and carried a Leslie Philips type moustache. His paunchy stomach poured over the stone coloured safari look-a-like long shorts. He had the posture of one who you just knew with certainty, was going to exude arrogance before he even opened his mouth. I wasn't wrong.

Unlike the other guests who always said hello when you passed them, he just nodded, nose in the air as if he was way above me to waste any words.

Halfway through my main course with Peter the owner sitting behind me on a sofa, I was deep into reading my next book and the first I was aware of Mr Arrogant was when a voice boomed out behind me shouting,

"I'm letting you formally know that I will be demanding 100% refund for every night I am without air-conditioning". Peter was obviously taken aback by this sudden arrival and outburst, and there was a brief pause followed by a soft Dutch accent,

"Excuse me?"

"I reported my air-conditioning not working this morning. You have had all day to do something about it, and you've done nothing. ABSOLUTELY NOTHING!"

"On the contrary sir, we've had the engineer out to look at it today and he needs to get a spare part, and he…"

"Well they should have got one" boomed the response before Peter finished speaking.

With an amazing calm Peter continued, "May I remind you sir that this is The Gambia. It is not always easy to get spare parts quickly"

"Then that's your problem, not mine. As I said, I want 100% refund for every night without air-conditioning. We paid for a package, and that package included air-conditioning, which we haven't got, so the package is not as described."

"I could change you to an alternative suite?"

"I don't want an alternative suite. We specifically wanted this one and you should have ensured that it was in full working order. Just thought I'd tell you formally," and Mr Arrogant stormed off back to his table.

He returned less than two minutes later.

"Oh, and by the way, I know for certain that the room beneath ours has a large stand-a-lone fan. I want that delivered to my room IMMEDIATELY!"

Ah-ha, I mused, being the invisible witness to this charade, so they've been snooping around looking into the rooms on the ground floor. I knew there was a good reason why I always requested first or second floor rooms. More seriously, I was wondering how the patron was going to respond to such a rude, loud and public outburst in his restaurant. Every guest and member of staff would have heard word for word, despite their body language pretending to be doing something else.

"I will arrange for the fan to be taken to your room immediately." Peter said very calmly, and then in a softer voice, "but I do not like your tone sir, and you will leave my hotel tomorrow."

I wanted to leap up, cheer and applaud the patron, as despite Mr Arrogant being ridiculously over the top and ignorant of Gambian culture, Peter hadn't stuck to the adage of "the customer is always right" and taken shit lying down from this obnoxious prat, nor had he matched him with shouting back, but he had very calmly and without raising his voice, told Mr Arrogant to leave the next day. Yeah! Mental high fives.

There was a silence before a slightly wobbly arrogant voice whimpered,

"But I have nowhere to go."

"I'll tell The Gambian Experience tomorrow and they will arrange something. Good night." And with this, Peter turned and walked off. The conversation was finished.

Day 3 – Hair-do

No lie in that day, and indeed an early start as Ay-ya was coming is to do my hair at 8.00am and I wanted to have breakfasted by then. As it turned out, I ate at 7.30am and Ay-ya turned up at 9.00am. I offered her a tea or juice, but she declined. She showed me the extensions she had bought, and explained in broken English that she had chosen ones that would work best for me. Black and gold. I was not convinced. She held them up against my hair and they looked awful. Perhaps she was colour blind? Perhaps they were the only ones they sold. I looked at the packet. It came from Japan and was a wedge of around three feet of polypropylene hair folded in half.

She opened the packet, and smiled,

"Good; no?" meaning yes. I felt it and it instantly reminded me of dolls hair from my childhood; thick plastic strands. Then I changed my mind, my dolls hair was much softer. I had downloaded a couple of photos from the internet to show her pictorially what I liked, in case the language barrier proved too much. She said that she understood, however after a few minutes phoned Jasmine who came to the room to confirm what she thought she understood. I then settled down on a cushion on the floor between Ay-ya's legs, and she started plaiting.

Her English was not great, however in the two and a half hours that followed, I learned that she was born in Banjul and that her mother lived with her younger sister and brother in Bansang, several hours away. Her father, who had been a doctor and posted to Bansang had died the previous year. She had one older sister who was married and who had never worked. Because of schooling and college, Ay-ya had remained in Banjul and had mainly been brought up by her grandmother with whom she was still living. She wasn't married. She had had a boyfriend until recently but had finished with him. She had studied IT at college and couldn't find a job, however her uncle who also worked at Ngala Lodge had found her a job in the kitchen. She worked from 3.00pm until 10.00pm and her speciality was making the dinner starters. She told me what the specials were for that evening, and one, a cocktail of prawn and butterfish with salad and lots of different dressings sounded extremely appealing. I said that I would chose that one for my dinner.

"I'm surprised that they don't have hairdressing on the menu of hotel services," I said along with hand gestures to aid comprehension, "or at least a plaiting service as I know that is popular with the tourists." She shrugged her shoulders as if to say she didn't understand either.

"Perhaps you could earn more money from hairdressing than working in the kitchens, or at the very least have some extra income."

"That would be nice," she replied "Will tell to my uncle." She also explained that she had a friend in Switzerland who worked in a salon where the money was very good and she had been trying to persuade Ay-Ya to join her. It took a while to work out what Ay-ya was saying as she pronounced "salon" as "shallon", but I got there in the end. She asked whether there were many shallons in England for African hairstyles, and I replied that I didn't know of any, but there were possibly some in African quarters that catered for the African styles. However, just as her mother had taught her how to plait hair, perhaps English Africans looked after each other within their communities rather than have formal "shallons". I said I didn't really know.

After completing the full head of hair, she started tying extensions of plastic hair on to the end of each plait. It took me a few minutes to realise what she was doing and then I gestured her to stop as I didn't really want to have black and gold plastic dreadlocks. I asked her to guide my hand to where my real hair finished and then I gestured to cut off the extensions at that point. I also got her to leave my fringe so that I could flick it back if I wanted to. I wasn't convinced that tight African plaits drawn back from my forehead would suit, however as I looked in the mirror at the finished style, I then wasn't convinced that I should have left the fringe, as it really did look quite odd sticking out on it's own with the rest of my hair in tight plaits against my skull. I made a mental note to cut my fringe shorter after she has gone. Her plaiting though was great and she had perfectly straight lines.

I wanted to send a couple of postcards. I knew anyway that I'd be at home at least three weeks before they arrived, but I still felt the need to send them sooner rather than later. People back home kind of "expected them".

At reception they had a choice of two postcards, both were of the hotel. One was just a black background with Ngala Lodge name written across the front in white, and the other was a picture of individual members of staff with Ngala Lodge across the top. Nah, I couldn't send those, I needed to get some "proper" cards, ones that gave a glimpse of "real" Gambia. Oh no, that meant a trip down the road again, running the gauntlet of kids with rats, an army of Velcro Men and over exuberant stall holders. It was going to much easier to get a taxi as they weren't that expensive. But first things first. It was lunchtime, I was hungry and The Clay Oven lay waiting only ten to fifteen minutes walk away according to the map.

Luckily as I stepped out of the compound and into the street, I turned right, away from the area I'd walked yesterday and headed away from kids with rats and Velcro Men. The red sandy road stretched out before me, yet in the distance I could see the left turn that would take me down to The Clay Oven. I passed a couple of men squatting on the other side of the road who shouted that they liked my Gambian hair style, and I waved and smiled back, though kept moving. The Clay Oven was just a short walk down a side street and within a few minutes I was there. My mouth was starting to water at the thought of the best authentic Indian food outside of India in the intimate Indian decorated room.

I was there but I didn't recognise it, which I found a little disappointing and disconcerting as I wasn't getting that warm "welcome home" feeling I always got when I ate there. I was greeted by an African waiter who showed me into the restaurant. Clothes were being dried, spread out on dusty grass in front of the restaurant, as one may expect to see in India, but I was especially disappointed that there wasn't the little old Indian chap with a big ivory smile to greet me.

I didn't recognise the interior of the restaurant at all. It was larger, at least three times as big and significantly more impersonal than my memory told me. However, on the way to the main restaurant I spied a small room off to the left and I wondered if that was the room I'd eaten in previously. It wasn't. It was very hot and sticky and the waiter showed me to a table underneath an air-conditioning unit. Whilst he fiddled with the switches to turn it on, I went through the now very familiar "where you from? How long you stay? Is this your first visit to Gambia?". I answered politely and at the end added that The Clay Oven was my favourite Indian restaurant outside of India, and that I first came 20 years ago.

"That will be the old place" said the waiter "we moved here 5 years ago."

Ah, so that at least explained why I didn't recognise it. I had never been here before. It is so weird how your memory tries to make sense out of something so unfamiliar yet you try hard to force the pieces of jigsaw together. I was relieved that it was a relocated restaurant and not the early signs of dementia, but also disappointed. The room was large, like a ballroom, with about fifty tables neatly set in rows. There were very few decorations and no obvious signs that it was indeed an Indian restaurant. I wanted the cosy, dark, intimate little restaurant that I recalled so fondly. The waiter was not even dressed for the role, wearing the same blue shirt and trousers that the security guards were wearing back at Ngala. Beads of sweat were running down his face, which didn't do a huge amount to enhance the ambience or appetite, and his eyes revealed that it was a real pain that I'd turned up for lunch. I was the only customer in this cavernous hall. Perhaps once I'd settled down and got a beer, a smartly dressed Indian with an authentic smile and demeanour would approach to take my order and the food would at least be as good as I remembered, even if the ambience wasn't. The waiter asked what I wanted to drink, and I ordered a large draught beer and bottle of water. He left me the menu and went off to fix my drinks.

I heard a snorting and phlegmy clearing of throat and turned to see another African behind the bar at the far end of the "ballroom". This was not a great start. Two African men serving in an Indian restaurant, one sweating profusely and the other snorting and coughing. I expected the chubby Indian owner to appear around the corner at any moment. He didn't. Indeed, throughout lunch I didn't see one Indian.

Prawn Shashlick followed by a spicy prawn dish served with basmati rice, a Paratha and a Clay Oven special Raita was ordered. The drinks arrived and I sat back with enormous expectation of the banquet to follow. I picked up the large beer to take a quaff, only to realise that it hasn't been properly chilled. In fact, it hadn't been chilled at all, and tasted like it had been outside all morning in the sun. Oh no, another disappointment. When the sweaty waiter returned with some Papadoms I told him that the beer wasn't cold and he just shrugged and uttered half an apology,

"The fridge isn't working," and he turned and headed back to the kitchens. Well, as I wasn't going to get a cold beer I may as well put up with this one, at least it was wet.

I'd hardly started the Popadom when the waiter arrived with

my starter. He'd just finished laying it out when he mumbled,

"Have to turn off air conditioning. Maintenance."

"No," I exclaimed, "you have to be joking, it's far too hot in here without the air conditioning." I wafted my serviette around to enhance the point I was making.

"I'll move you to a table in the corner, and then I can open the window on both sides and you'll have some fresh air." He showed me to the alternative table carrying my rapidly cooling starter, and his face told the real story as if it were burned on with a pyrography pen. His boss has said something along the lines of "You put the air conditioning on for the sake of one customer!! Have you any idea how much that costs!! Turn it off immediately and move her to a table near a window. Make some excuse about maintenance or similar."

Once settled at the table, he opened a window and the breeze that followed wouldn't even have moved a feather, yet it seemed to move the offensive smell of sewers from outside. Remember, it was one hundred degrees outside, very humid, and I was about to eat hot and spicy food. Despite the welcome and service being about the worst I'd ever experienced in a restaurant, the food was indeed up to its excellent standard, even if it was washed down with a warm beer.

The main course was served only a few seconds after I'd put down my knife and fork from the starter. It was abundantly clear that although they were open, they really couldn't be bothered with customers at lunchtime outside the main tourist season. The meal came to an end and I didn't want to hang around longer than necessary, so I asked for the bill. I was a little curt when I asked for it, however when I added "the food was excellent," that was absolutely truthful.

The bill came to one thousand Dalasi exactly with the service charge included, probably because they knew that no tip would be forthcoming otherwise. I handed over a credit card.

" Sorry, but Mastercard machine not working"

"No problem, I have a Visa card also", and I started to fish in my purse.

"Sorry madam, it same machine as Mastercard. You pay cash." Although I had the cash in my purse, I was reluctant to use it as I needed it to see me through the week, and on principle, I determined that he would take my card.

"Why didn't you tell me before I even ordered food that your machine was out of order?"

"Sorry. Cash only," as even more beads of sweat formed on his brow.

"Where does it say that you are a cash only restaurant or that today you are only taking cash?" I demanded. Of course it was written nowhere.

"Cash only. You have to pay cash."

"Do you have an old paper type manual machine?"

"No. Sorry".

"Then I think you need to call the manager please"

He scuffled off and returned quite swiftly, not with the manager, but with an old paper style card swiper. I gave him my card, but he couldn't work out where to put it, and his first three attempts ended up with nothing more than a pile of crumpled dockets.

"One moment," and he sloped off to find assistance. A third African appeared. He was not in the same casual blue, but was wearing a dark suit with shirt and tie. He was obviously more senior, but still didn't have the air of "boss" about him. I watched as he also struggled with the machine, shredding more paper. I'd had enough as the pile of aborted crumpled foils massed around the desk. I took the machine off him, inserted the card in the correct place and swiped.

I had to pay in English pounds as the dockets were processed by an American bank that wouldn't accept Dalasi. About £23.80 in English money, so I wrote this on the swiped docket. I noticed that it hasn't properly swiped my number. Part of me felt like leaving it and letting them sort out the free meal they'd effectively given me, however my conscience was greater than my desire to teach them a lesson, so before he peeled off the carbon paper I wrote the card number clearly at the top of the page. I packed the receipt away along with all the aborted attempts. Although I doubted that even Turing would have been able to decipher anything from the scraps of paper, when it comes to credit cards you can never be too careful. I left, and couldn't even bring myself to say thank you.

As I walked back to the hotel, I told myself that I wouldn't be using the Clay Oven ever again, and I would just have to remember with fondness the charming old place of the past, with it's friendly and excellent service. I mused over what may have happened. Perhaps the old boy died and an African businessman bought out the business? Realising that it lived or died on its authenticity, he probably retained the Indian chefs, but dispensed with the waiters, giving those jobs to friends and family. Or perhaps the old boy died and a greedy son thought that because they were fully booked every night the key was to have a larger place at the expense of retaining the authentic atmosphere. My imagination was running wild when I heard a car tooting behind me. It was the manager of The Clay Oven, looking very flustered.

"Stop! Please stop!" he panted. "My boss won't accept the paper because you wrote on it. If you jump in the car I'll take you back to the hotel, and perhaps someone there knows how to work the machine."

"The hotel is only up there" I pointed. "I'll see you at reception" and carried on walking. I wasn't about to jump into anyone's car.

At the Ngala reception, it was clear that the flustered manager was expecting even more abortive attempts as he not only had the machine in his hand, but about 5 or 6 blank dockets also.

The chap on reception was just so cool. He took the machine with the suave sophistication of James Bond, deftly placed my card in the correct place, eased in a slip of paper and swiftly swiped the card in one movement. I had now paid for my meal. The difference between the two was not just chalk and cheese, but primary school versus PhD level.

As soon as The Clay Oven manager had crawled back into his hole, I asked reception for a taxi to take me down to the local shops to get some postcards. It was only a few minutes drive down to a little kiosk shop. The lad behind the counter was smart, well dressed and I quickly discovered, polite, well educated and had lived in the UK for two years. He also knew British geography better than most Brits. When people asked me "Where in England?" I'd said Newcastle because it was the largest city in the Northeast and therefore stood a chance of being heard of. Also, there was for some unfathomable reason, an instant connection to football. When I told the young man "Newcastle" his eyes lit up and told me that he had had a great week's holiday in Scarborough. He was in the UK for two years studying in Bournemouth.

What a shame that such an eloquent and clearly bright young man was working in a shack shop.

Back to the hotel to write the postcards and to carry on reading.

I took the completed postcards down to reception to get some stamps. The young male behind the counter, who was standing in for the main receptionist, had to write me a receipt. The bill was only 90 Dalasi, but I guessed they had to account for every penny. He slowly and laboriously wrote out the receipt, tore off the top copy for me, removed the carbon paper and then looked at the pad quizzically. The carbon copy hadn't come out. His copy was just a blank piece of paper. I picked up my receipt and folded it in half to fit into my purse, and as soon as I saw the back of it, I realised that he'd had the carbon paper the wrong way around. When he returned from the back office, I showed him the back of my receipt and turned over the carbon paper. He smiled as if it was a game of patter-cake and turned the carbon paper over again.

"No", I said "You need to have the carbon paper over this way." He still looked confused. I scribbled in the corner of the pad with my finger nail, just a few scratches and then lifted the carbon paper to show it working. There was a split second of bemusement, then I saw the penny drop and a grin spread across his face. He now knew how to use carbon paper.

At dinner I was a little surprised to see Mr Arrogant and his partner dinning. So they hadn't been kicked out after all. Some apologies and agreements must have passed between him and Peter, because this evening he was as timid as a mouse and as quiet as the dead. He talked in whispers not shouts. He was a man subdued. Well done Peter.

I was the talk of the restaurant that evening because of my hair style. The staff trickled out of the kitchen to tell me how much they liked it. Ah-ya was working and came out sheepishly with a broad smile. Everyone knew she had done it and patted her on the back in recognition of a job well done.

When I was in The Gambia 25 years previously, there were braiding ladies everywhere – at the hotel, on the beach and out and about in the streets. You just couldn't avoid them. Yet this time I had had to actively seek out a plaiter and by the attention I was receiving and the praise Ay-ja was getting, it was clearly not as common an occurrence as in the past.

I was served an extra large portion of starters. Prawns and Butterfish.Delicious.

Day 4 – Delightful Company

This was definitely going to be a chill out day, so after breakfast I found a lounger with a parasol in the garden area and settled myself down. Richard and Sarah, a pleasant and relaxed English couple I'd said hello to a few times, came over and asked me if I wanted to join them for dinner. They were planning to go to the Butchers Shop which offered a wide range and variety of cuisines. I hesitated for a moment, partly because I didn't want to intrude on someone else's holiday, which of course was crazy because they'd asked me, and partly because it went through my mind that I was on half board and this would mean additional expenditure, but I quickly said yes, as it would be pleasant to do something different. The food was generally excellent at Ngala, however I had realised after just a few days that it didn't matter what you ordered for your main course, it always came with creamed spinach, mashed potato and a slice of courgette with mashed carrot on top.

We agreed to meet at 7.00pm by the reception area, and I passed the morning reading and writing. I finished the Zoe Strachen book "Ever Been in Love". On the one hand, the book didn't totally resolve at the end, but on the other hand it felt as if there was sufficient left open to either let the mind consider possibilities, or Zoe to write a sequel. I'd really enjoyed it, so I hoped it was the latter. I had started planning writing my own psychological thriller, with a working title of "Toxic Man" but was still struggling with a suitable ending, so I brainstormed some possibilities, from the male protagonist dying a horrible illness, to the two main characters living happily ever after. I actually came up with an ending that leaves it open for a sequel, so was satisfied with the progress.

I went to the Lodge restaurant for lunch. Richard and Sarah were there and I commented on the especially large crows they had out here, nodding to two large birds perched on the bird table just a matter of feet outside the open restaurant window. Then I did a double take. They were not crows, but vultures. Vultures eating from a standard bird table.

The afternoon was spent reading. I'd treated myself to a Kindle before I came away, but wasn't certain that I'd take to it, as there was something special and intimate about the physical feel of a page between ones' fingers, the slight aroma of paper and that you can cuddle up with a book in bed, flexing it's cover to suit your position. However, they were still sufficiently new and different that if it didn't work out, I could sell it for a reasonable price on Ebay. I had downloaded a few free books before I came away and was astounded not only how easy it was to use but how quickly, literally seconds, it took to download each book. I had however also packed half a dozen paperbacks just in case I didn't gel with the Kindle and then felt as if I was stuck with nothing to read. It came with no instructions, so I had to fiddle with the menu and work things out myself. Different font options, how to bookmark a page and how to make notes if you wanted to. It was incredibly intuitive and didn't take long to try out all the options, and indeed the sheer mechanics of "getting to know your Kindle" started to build a confidence with it. First impressions were therefore extremely positive.

I opened it for the first time to actually read something and started to read a trashy holiday novel, a legal thriller. Within just a few pages I was used to the feel, holding it, the ease of reading it, lack of sun glare that had previously concerned me, and very quickly decided that it was indeed an excellent purchase. As I got up around teatime to head back to the room I spotted Mr Arrogant and his weathered partner sunbathing on the decking by the sea. She was topless, which wasn't a pretty sight.

Early evening, I took a quick shower, changed and met up with Richard and Sarah. It was only a fifteen minute walk to the restaurant and still only dusk, so we decided to walk to the restaurant and then get a taxi back.

The restaurant was in almost total darkness save for a few candles. The manager stepped forward and apologised profusely that the generator was down and so they had no electricity for air-conditioning or lighting. Richard and Sarah seemed a little embarrassed by this, as it was their choice of restaurant, especially as the same thing had happened to them the previous evening and they had assumed it would have been fixed by then. I just laughed it off as part of the Gambian experience, and it broke the ice. We chose a table by the open sides so that we'd at least get a little breeze.

As they had eaten there before, they highly recommend the captain fish served in a banana leaf, spiced with cumin, garlic and coriander. The spicy grilled tiger prawns were also recommended, although they were only available as a main dish. Ordering the food proved a little difficult as we asked for three half size portions of prawns to start with followed by the captain fish in the banana leaf. They were right out of banana leaves and found the suggested concept of using silver foil instead, too far removed to comprehend. The waiter had several trips to and from the kitchen and on the third trip, returned announcing proudly that they could indeed cook the spicy captain fish in silver foil instead. Then came the prawn saga. Firstly, we discovered that they didn't have tiger prawns that evening just the regular prawns, and they couldn't cook the dish as a starter, only as a main course. Richard quickly chipped in and said that we'd have 2 portions of the main course prawns as a starter, but with three plates. The waiter kept insisting that we couldn't have half portions, and we kept replying that we didn't want half portions, just two full portions and an extra plate. The waiter than nodded furiously with a big smile. He had grasped the order,

"Two tiger prawn and a half portion of captain fish? Yes?"

"No!" we all shrieked together with huge grins broadening our faces and added in unison, "three full portions of captain fish." The waiter nodded and disappeared as we giggled between ourselves that we had no idea what we'd be served. However, we were indeed served two full portions of prawns with an extra plate followed by three full portions of captain fish. We had asked for chips, but were served rice, but what the hell, most of the order was pretty damned close to what we wanted, and it was all served with genuine Gambian hospitality. I'll also add that their regular sized prawns were larger than I would have expected for tiger prawns, so their tiger prawns when they had them in, must be the size of lobsters. The food was nothing short of excellent. Definitely fresh, but also with exactly the right balance of herbs and spices to tang the tongue yet not disguise the underlying fish flavours. I didn't mind that there was no air-conditioning or lighting and that we were eating by candlelight, the restaurant was a first class choice, with service a million miles better that The Clay Oven.

Richard and Sarah were a great couple and excellent company. They had lived and worked in many parts of the world. For several years Richard had been a senior negotiator for a well known global food company. In addition to this they were very well travelled, and most of the evening was spent swapping, mainly humorous, travel tales. I also found a new country to add to my bucket list – Cuba. I'd not included it before because a friend who had been there had commented that the Cubans, although having happy smiley faces, and being very welcoming, actually saw all tourists as dollars on legs. Richard and Sarah however, painted a very different picture. They really enjoyed their holiday, and found the people genuinely happy and eager to please. They told me that everyone in Cuba earned the same wage regardless of qualifications, which created an equal society and therefore no obvious displays of opulence, but equally no abject poverty either. They had used a taxi driver during their stay in Havana who had qualified as a doctor, however had decided to be a taxi driver instead as he found it fascinating talking to visitors and learning about other cultures. Furthermore, he may have received the same formal salary as when he was a doctor, but he was also tipped quite lucratively. Perhaps then this was proof that tourists were indeed dollars on legs. It didn't matter. They painted such a colourful picture of their particular holiday, that Cuba was from that point destined for my bucket list.

Richard told me that he loved haggling and tried to get a deal on anything and everything he purchased, including back home. Even estate agents. He said he didn't bother with the two percent of purchase fee, but would say to a potential agent "We want to sell, you want us to sell, so we'll go for a lower asking price, however we are only going to pay you five thousand pounds." The agents generally bought it.

Although he was now retired, he still seemed to have his fingers in many pies. They were clearly not short of money, lived comfortably and travelled well, but were not in the least ostentatious about it, and indeed incredibly down to earth and well grounded. One of my favourite tales from the evening was from Richard, who after telling them my tale of Velcro Man, said that they'd had a similar experience, but with two Velcro Men, both wanting to be a guide, both wanting to be a friend. As they'd left the market to get a taxi back to the hotel, Richard decided to give them some money, even though they had done nothing but pester them for twenty minutes, so he took out a one hundred Dalasi note, tore it in half, gave them each a half and said with a smile "sort it out between yourselves." He had a moment of panic when he thought guards may appear from nowhere to arrest him for defacing the currency, but instead he left two disgruntled Velcro's as his taxi pulled away, trying to work out what they would each do with half a bank note.

Richard and Sarah were in The Gambia for the opening of a new classroom in a school. They had been over in December for a holiday, and had agreed to donate some money for a school to build a third classroom, and now they'd been invited to the opening of this new classroom, which was why they were back in The Gambia. I'd seen them the previous afternoon when they'd returned, exhausted from the opening ceremony and had asked them what it was like.

"The ceremony lasted four hours," Richard said as he rolled his eyes.

"When we saw the programme, it looked like a lot of speeches and dancing," chipped in Sarah.

"Which lasted four hours," added Richard.

"The taxi driver told us to have our cameras ready when we entered the compound, and he was right. Everyone had turned out to greet us with flowers. The children, in their best school uniforms, with immensely happy smiling faces, were singing. It was truly amazing and it brought a lump to my throat," continued Sarah in animated excitement.

"Yes – and it took four hours."

"We were then seated in two special chairs which made us feel like a king and queen, and the ceremony started."

"Which lasted four hours."

"All of the elders of the nearby villages were there, and they each had to give the new classroom their blessing."

"Which is why it took four hours."

"Were you the only westerners to attend the ceremony, or were there others," I chipped in after stopping laughing at Richard's rolling eyes over the length of the event.

"Yes, just us two."

Assuming that other contributors hadn't been bothered to attend, I added

"Gosh. I bet the locals thought that you'd bought the whole classroom."

"We did," said Richard in the most modest and self-effacing manner. "When we were over in December, we'd visited the school, which wasn't far from our hotel. We got chatting with the headmaster, who was telling us about the pupils, their academic achievements, and difficulties the school faced. We were somewhat shocked by how tightly the children were packed into the classroom and the headmaster told us that he took as many children as he could, but that there was a long waiting list and they only had two school rooms. I asked how much a new schoolroom cost, and the headmaster told me. We liked him. He never once asked for any money or help, he was just pleased to be giving as many children as possible, a decent education. After leaving the school, we went for a drink to cool down, and chatted about our experience of visiting the school. Although the amount of money required to build a new classroom was relatively small by British standards, it was a massive mountain to climb for the Gambians. So, I went back to the school, sought out the headmaster and just said, *you can book the builders*. When we returned home, I arranged the payment transfer, and now they have a new schoolroom."

When I'd jokingly said that the locals would have thought that they'd paid for it all, as they were the only westerners to attend the ceremony, they actually had. Yet there was no bragging about it. No pretension. Indeed, I doubt they would have told me had I not been curious to know more about the project. Apart from the fact that I'd already decided that they were a really decent couple, with fascinating international tales to tell, they just went up further in my estimation. I also wished that I had that sort of money to do something philanthropic also.

We took a taxi back to the hotel and it was nearly 11.00pm and I'd been going to bed at 9.30pm, yet it had been such an enjoyable and stimulating evening, the time had just whizzed past.

Although I generally kept myself to myself on holiday, and did people watching from a distance, there was definitely merit in spending at least one evening with strangers. They must have spotted something in me that suggested I'd be a good evening guest. They had been great company and I wanted to learn to spot the same in others, as an evening with them had enriched the holiday significantly.

Day 5 – Safari in Senegal

The pick up was 8.00am for the day trip to Senegal and the safari. I was down in the restaurant promptly at 7.30am for breakfast. There was an elderly English gentleman whom I'd seen a couple of times but not spoken to, who was already eating. I sat at the table next to him and we started chatting.

He had a soft lilting Irish accent, was around seventy years old but still with a full head of wispy white hair, wiry thin and a face that could tell many stories. He was wearing crumpled white chinos and shirt, both of which looked like they had been worn for several years and never seen an iron. He had a battered straw hat by his side. He looked like the old colonial sort and would not have been out of place cracking peanuts and drinking gin slings in Raffles. I discovered that he worked for a major international aid charity, had done so for nearly forty years, and now specifically looked after vaccination administration for West Africa. Although his base was Dakar, he spent most of his time travelling from country to country. He'd left England in 1969, and hadn't been back since. I asked if he had anywhere that he called home, as it seemed he spent most of his time travelling around.

As we chatted, I found one thing a little disturbing. Having worked for World Vision for two years part time, I understood the workings of international aid agencies, and certainly at World Vision, every penny counted and they prided themselves on the low ratio of spend on admin, with the vast majority of funds really going towards their good causes. It transpired that this elderly gentleman had several places he called home. He had an apartment in Dakar, a house in France, and a further apartment in Switzerland. I thought that he must have a fair amount of money, not only to maintain three properties, but also to visit them. He was also staying at one of the most expensive places in Gambia, probably on expenses. Of course, he may have been fortunate enough to have inherited wealth but I did wonder about the financial integrity of this particular aid agency if they could afford to pay him a salary sufficient to maintain the three properties and put him up in expensive hotels, when there were perfectly reasonable three and four star hotels in The Gambia.

I was then off for the day and was the last to be picked up by the mini bus. My heart sank. There was one couple around my age, sitting at the back away from everyone else, and a dozen "kids" in their twenties, three lads and nine girls, and they were exceptionally loud. Most were talking over each other which meant that the decibels were raised just so that they could hear each other and participate in all conversations at once. Most of the girls were wearing low top T-shirts, or vests, leaving little to the imagination, and most sported various tattoos and piercings. I picked up on snippets of conversation.

"God, you were so wasted last night."

"That couple on the next table had a real f*****g sense of humour failure. I think they were out for a cosy night for two."

"The funniest bit was when you climbed onto the table and started singing."

"Nah, the funniest f****g bit was when you f******g suggested we break plates like we did in that f*****g Greek place last year.

"What about that old English cow who told us we were a disgrace. Bet she hasn't had a day of fun in her whole pigging life."

I zoned out of the conversation, but the one person my eyes and ears were immediately drawn to was a girl, smaller than five feet, short spiky dyed bright orange hair, a piercing in her nose, chin, and several on both ears, and she was LOUD! Oh wow, I was in for an interesting day.

The tour guide for the day handed round a board, and asked us to write our names, passport numbers and occupations on the list, as this would be required when we crossed the border into Senegal. It went round the bus and I was the last to have it. I glanced down the list to get a feel for my fellow travellers, and reading the list of occupations, saw that one of them had written vicar. That must be a joke. It was by the name Charlie. I looked up and sought out the three lads. There was one with tight dark curly hair and a swarthy gypsy appearance, enhanced by the three gold earrings in each ear. He was leaning over one of the seats trying to read something the girls were giggling at. The second had lank, greasy hair tied back in a pony tail, a vest sporting the name of a band I hadn't heard of and was gesticulating wildly as he described the revelries of the previous evening. The third, with short wavy blond hair was sitting slightly apart from the other and gazing out of the window at the passing truck, piled high with furniture and being pulled by a single ox. I reckoned that this must be Charlie, the vicar, if for no other reason than he looked like Mikey from university, who had become a missionary.

Most of the occupations were written down as students, and I wondered how these kids could afford such a holiday, especially as they were staying at The Sunset Hotel, which wasn't cheap.

All the way to the Banjul ferry they were loud, and however hard I tried not to listen to their conversations, as I didn't want them to think I was eavesdropping, I just couldn't avoid it, indeed I doubted I'd have been able to avoid it even with ear plugs and headphones. So I quickly gathered that they'd had a few wild nights out in Gambia, upset a few people in restaurants, danced on tables and suffered numerous hangovers between them. They were all from the same area back home and were linked by having participated in a Gambian school project, and were now combining visiting the project with a holiday. They seemed to have travelled in pairs, however small sub groups had formed. One pair of blondes, although unrelated, looked like clones. They had their hair piled on top of their heads in a 1960's style, and grabbed a smoke at every opportunity. They huddled together most of the time and lacked confidence beyond their comfy friendship.

We arrived at the ferry and the bustle of everyday activities. Older ladies were sitting silently watching the world go by, chewing bark or roots, legs splayed open which would have been somewhat revealing if it wasn't for their long colourful batik skirts. They eyed us shiftily, and my finger itched to take a photograph, however their suspicious eyes were saying, "Mama, you even hint at pointing that camera in my direction and I'll be wanting 100 Dalasi." Many passengers were carrying their wares over to Senegal. Huge baskets of fruit which I doubted I could lift off the ground, let alone balance on my head, and yet they carried them as if they were supporting nothing more than a slightly heavy hat. Bicycles and mopeds were overloaded with bags and boxes of stuff, but probably the most unusual sight was a chap carrying a fridge on his head. There was a queue of sorts for the ferry, yet despite its millionth journey across to Barra, they loaded the people and trucks with the disorganisation as if they were doing it for the first time.

Our guide for the day, Doodoo who told us that this translates to "Darling" and had no similarity with the colloquial English use of the word, encouraged us to go up the stairs at the side of the main cargo deck and find a seat, as there would be standing room only very quickly.

During the crossing, shoe shine boys tried to clean our shoes. As I was wearing trainers and I knew they were going to get very dusty, there was little point. A fat lady waddled around the deck selling packets of frozen water and juices, which reminded me a little of the old fashioned triangular Jublies I drank as a child.

One of the "kids group" sat next to me as there was no room on the bench with her friends. She had a sulky, sullen look and on the one hand looked as if she had led a sheltered life and that this was her first venture into the big wide world alone, yet she sported a large rose tattoo on her shoulder and vine tattoos on both arms starting at the wrist and creeping up the arm like poison ivy. She looked like the kind of girl who only had tattoos to fit in with her peers, however had been a little over exuberant with their usage, possibly to prove that she really, really wanted to be part of the gang.

I tried to start up a conversation with her, but she clearly felt uncomfortable in the presence of this "old lady". I got as far as discovering that she was studying mental health at college, so I told her that my degree was in psychology, to ease her into a conversation, but her body language was screaming "I want to be with my friends, talking about last night's party – not sitting here chatting with this batty woman! I am sooo out of my comfort zone!" A Gambian left the bench behind me and she took the opportunity to escape and scuttle back to the safety of the group.

The crossing took about two hours and as there was nothing much of note to watch, I read my book for most of the journey.

Leaving the ship, we were jostled through a dirty, smelly street past a row of shack shops, with high pestering to buy wooden masks, giraffe carvings, sunglasses, baseball caps and sweets. The vendors shouted that the children at the border liked to have sweets so it was good to buy some there whilst we had the opportunity. They were mainly packets of little lollies, so I bought a couple of packets, and then we were led through the stinking market to the toilets, which we are told were the only ones for the next hour or two. The ladies toilet door didn't stay closed, so the kids were taking turns to lean on the rusty metal door, which otherwise would have swung open, whilst their friends used the facilities. There was of course no toilet paper, and none of them had paper hankies or wet ones, so I handed out mine as they left the bog hole. Only one hung around to push against the door when it was my turn. It was the petite orange spikey haired girl.

"Thanks," I said when I emerged and let the breath out that I had been holding since entering the hut.

"Cool," she answered, "I couldn't leave you sitting there having a pee with all the world watching." We both laughed.

"Wot's yer name?"

"Susan," I replied, "and yours?"

"Charlie. I was christened Charlotte, but have used Charlie since back when I can't remember."

Charlie. The list came back to me. Vicar. As we strolled back to join the others I asked hesitatingly,

"Charlie. You're not the vicar are you?"

"Yeah. That's me, although I'm actually only a curate at the moment, but hoping to get my own parish in a year or two. I share myself between 3 churches."

You could have knocked me down with a feather. Just goes to show how wrong you can be by appearances.

Back through the putrid market, we climbed into an open sided army type truck, our vehicle for the remainder of the day, and headed off to Senegal.

Once in the truck, Charlie was trying to galvanise her friends into playing games. I-Spy, guess the celebrity and so on. Nobody really wanted to play and the games fizzled out in the first couple of rounds, so Charlie punctuated the pauses with singing. She had a rough throaty voice as if she'd been gargling razor blades for years, and at her high constant volume it was like having your hearing scoured with sandpaper. I imagined that the volume was especially turned up because she was used to preaching from a pulpit.

Gambia on the other side of the river looked pretty much like, well, Gambia on the other side of the river. We slowed down going through a small village, bustling with people and traffic, and came to a stop. Coming from the opposite direction was an amusing sight. It was a car of about the size of a UK SUV, and had five goats on the roof each tethered like a dog to the roof rack bars at either side. I fleetingly wondered how many lose their footing, slide off the roof and hang themselves. I grabbed my camera and - click. That was when all hell let loose.

The reason we had stopped was because we were at a police check point where it was illegal to take photos. There were no obvious signs that this was a police stop, just a small stone shack at the side of the road. There was a tiny "police check point" sign at the other side of the road, however at the time of the photo, this was obscured by the goat-mobile. A policeman came rushing up to the side of the truck, gesticulating wildly and screaming at our guide. It transpired that he saw me taking the photo and wanted my camera. The guide only then explained that I shouldn't be taking photos near a police station, to which I replied, that I was taking a picture of the goats, pointing to them as they were now alongside our truck. I also told him that I was aware one shouldn't take photos near a police station, however, and I waved my arms around, where was the sign? How was I to know? Doodoo explained this to the policeman, who carried on screaming and waving his arms around in the air.

"Tell him I'll delete the photo," I said, but the policeman was having none of it. He wanted me down from the truck and into the police station. I clambered over the side of the truck, the kids now silent for the first time since the hotel pick up, when Charlie piped up and asked if I wanted any of them to come with me for moral support. I appreciated the gesture, but said I'd be okay.

Doodoo and I crossed the street to the stone shack, which turned out to be the "police station". The original policeman was still shouting at me and pointing to the camera. The message was very clear despite me not understanding a word he was saying. I carefully wrapped the camera strap around my wrist to prevent the policeman from grabbing it from me, and then slowly turned it on. I'd seen enough movies to know that you don't make any sudden movements in situations like this. I showed him the picture of the goats and you couldn't even see a single stone of the police station. He then pointed to the lower right hand corner of the picture. Literally, right in the bottom corner there was a very tiny splash of yellow. It was his jacket elbow and I had to delete the picture. The camera remained welded to my wrist throughout all of this as I wasn't going to risk him taking the camera off me or making me delete all the photos taken so far.

He was now satisfied. His elbow had suitably been deleted from my camera, along with the great photo of the goats, and I was allowed to get back up into the truck. One of the kids said,

"Wow! That was pretty scary! I thought he was going to shoot you." Clearly a little over-melodramatic, however, when I looked at their faces I could see that at least half of them thought it was a real possibility. I grinned and just said,

"Shame. It was a bloody good photo."

We carried on for another five miles and reached the border with Senegal. Doodoo was clearly excited on our behalf that we were about to get a different country stamp in our passports, but what a farce. He collected our passports, all open on the page with the Gambia entry stamp, and we remained in the truck while he went to immigration control. During the half hour wait the truck was bombarded by ladies selling mangos and children selling packets of cashew nuts. Of course there were also children shouting for sweets, having been conditioned into this by the sellers back in Barra. Some of the children just reached up and grabbed sweets out of offering hands, trying to grab as many as their little hands would hold. Only a few stood patiently, waiting for their turn and then saying thank you for the receipt of just one lolly. Although my first two handfuls of lollies were distributed fairly randomly, I was keen that two little girls and a boy who were too small to reach up to the lorry, got their share. A slightly older boy stood at the edge of the children and I gestured to him that I wanted to give the little children some sweets, so he came forwards and picked them up one at a time lifting them up to my hand for their share. They each gave me a massive broad smile, as they usually got no sweets at all. The greedy girl in the middle, who already had four lollies in her hand was trying to reach for the little ones lollies. Thankfully the older boy and me were communicating telepathically and were determined that the little ones would have their lollies. As we were parked some way from the crossing patrol, I was able to take some photos without fear of losing my camera.

Doodoo returned to the truck with the stamped passports. Not one single official either counted the number of people in the truck or checked faces against photos. We could have been a truck load of illegal immigrants, and this whole inactivity took over half an hour. Doodoo however was ecstatic because he had got a new country stamp in our passports.

It was only about another five miles down the road when we reached the safari reserve. It wasn't a zoo, but equally it wasn't the wilds of Africa either. Having safaried in Kenya, where albeit the reserves are geared up for tourism, at least the national park areas were around one hundred and fifty thousand hectares each, so you did at least feel as if you were in the heart of Africa. This reserve was only one thousand hectares and was marked by a high wire mesh perimeter, so it did feel a little as if you were entering Longleat or Woburn and not embarking on a true safari.

We had an hour's drive around the reserve, stopping in places to alight and take photographs, and we got to see everything within the reserve except the rhino, which apparently hadn't been seen for a few days. There were zebra, giraffe, water buffalo, wart hogs, ostrich and a range of different deer – ibis, élan and so on. At one point I spotted a white vulture, a different type to those seen near the hotel and wanted to get a photo, but Doodoo insisted that there was a better picture ahead. He thought that I wanted to photograph the wart hogs, but by the time I'd explained it was a vulture, the bird had flown away and I missed the opportunity.

During the journey around the reserve, one of the girls spotted a Praying Mantis on the back of a seat. She popped it onto her hand and stretched out her arm showing it to everyone. Apart from Craig, the missionary lookalike, the rest of the kids squealed as if a mass murderer had suddenly alighted the lorry, or at the very least, the girl had a black widow spider crawling up her arm, and they tumbled over themselves trying to make as much distance between themselves and the Mantis. I was in the seat in front of the girl with the Mantis, and wanted to take a photo, however with the bumpy track I ended up taking about 20 photos to get just one in reasonable focus. The other kids didn't return to their seats until the Mantis was out of the truck and happily returned to its natural habitat.

Back in the main compound of the reserve, where you could buy snacks, drinks and souvenirs, there were two caged hyenas. I didn't think I'd ever seen a hyena in the flesh before, not even in a zoo. They were much bigger than I would have thought, about the size of a large Great Dane, but still with the silly faces which make them look more cartoon like than real. But they were real, and they were vicious. They were both male, their penises swishing low as they alternated between sniffing deeply of each others bum or throwing themselves against the wire fence in the hope of catching a tourist for lunch.

There was a horrible stench of rotting meat around the cage, and then I spotted the half eaten Élan. The hyenas can eat a whole Élan in just two to three days between them. Any dead animals found in the reserve were fed to the hyenas. Although native to West Africa, they are not allowed inside the reserve for rather obvious reasons and although ideally they would have been in a separate compound rather than a cage, despite it's large size, it was exciting to see them close up. Instinctively I would prefer them to be wild and free, clearing up after the circle of life has left other animals taken by old age or sickness, but it just couldn't work within this small reserve as it wouldn't take long for it to be devoid of animals.

We had lunch at the reserve, cold chicken with salad and bread and I took a few photos of exceptionally colourful magpies, their blue more iridescent than back in the UK, and then we headed back towards The Gambia. Border control took less than ten minutes on the return journey, and although we slowed down, we were not required to stop at the police border as on the way out.

Once again we waded through the rotting vegetation in the market to get to the ferry, but this time there was no hanging about and we could walk straight on as there was no queuing. However, there was a large school party occupying all of the seats, so we had to sit on the hard, rusty, flaking deck. There was no chivalry amongst the Gambian children to give up their seat for elders, nor did their teacher encourage them to do so. I had no doubt that Doodoo would have sent them scattering if we wanted a seat, but we all said we were okay, hunkered down on our bit of rust, and after all it was only a two hour crossing so we could get up and stretch our legs when we wanted. I saw a wooden dug out boat packed fuller than a tin of sardines pull alongside. It was an alternative to the ferry. It only took twenty five minutes to cross and cost just fifty Dalasi, however it would be an extremely bumpy and uncomfortable crossing. The other downside was that the jetty was too high for embarkation or disembarkation, so there were teams of people wading out from the beach to the little anchored boat, giving people a piggy-back to the shore.

Our ferry continued to fill up to the point that if we wanted to stand and stretch our legs there was not much room to do so. Eventually we set off and I fell into conversation with some of the kids, who were fascinated to hear about my Come Dine With Me television experience. Suddenly I wasn't a boring old lady anymore, but someone with street cred, as of course these kids lapped up any prospect of meeting someone with their fifteen minutes of fame. The episode hadn't been aired yet, but they knew about it because when we saw the zebras earlier in the day, I couldn't help but ask if any of them had ever eaten zebra. It was fair to say that they hadn't! Initially they were disgusted at the thought, however once I'd explained that I'd actually been served zebra during one of the dinners, their disgust over eating zebra rapidly transformed into fascination about Come Dine With Me. I told them as much as I was allowed to before airing, and also just enough that I didn't spoil it for them if they wanted to watch it. About half of the kids had realised that I wasn't the boring old biddy after all, and indeed they invited me out that evening to join them. Having heard their tales earlier of getting pissed, climbing on tables and dancing until dawn, I politely declined. Craig even said,

"Susan fits in really well with us. I like Susan – she's cool!",
and gave me a big hug. However, there were still half the kids
though, who felt uncomfortable with anyone outside of their
immediate group, and found it difficult to know when I was being
serious and when I was having a bit of funny banter.

I suddenly looked up. Although we'd departed the port half
an hour ago, we didn't seem to be making much progress, and
actually we were going nowhere because we were stuck on a
sandbank. The ferry was not only massively overloaded with
people and vehicles, but the one huge lorry on board, was
carrying scrap metal, and we were simply too heavy. We
couldn't go forward and equally we couldn't go back to offload.
We were stuck. There were several deck hands running around
trying to look like they knew what they were doing, whilst their
faces told all, with looks somewhere between clueless and
panic.

After about thirty minutes stuck on the sandbank, I heard the
sound of a large engine and a JCB appeared around the corner
of the ferry, moving very gingerly and using its scoop to
determine the safe depth it could move forward to before
sinking into the silt or toppling over. Satisfied with the depth, the
operator lifted the scoop and pushed against the side of the
ferry to try and shift it off the sandbank. One may have thought
that this was the first time it had happened, because of the
chaos amongst the crew and the chances of it happening in the
first place, however the speed with which the JCB was available
and galvanised into action, I sort of reckoned that it was a
regular occurrence, and typical of Gambia. Rather than consider
limiting the load of the ship, they just had the JCB on standby. It

gave the back of the ferry two large pushes, and it appeared that we were moving. Yes, they had definitely done this before. But wait a moment...we were going nowhere other than round in a circle, and the JCB retreated to the shore. We stopped moving. About thirty minutes passed with nothing happening, and the crew just looking helpless without a clue of what to try next. At one point it looked like they were going to move everyone aft to take the weight off the front, but thankfully that didn't happen, as it could have caused the ferry to topple over. Furthermore, possibly because we were so tightly packed in, there wouldn't be much to gain by making us shuffle a few paces forward. The rear had no safety guard, just a thin white chain casually looped across the gap. The two cars parked closest to the rear were asked to move forward to get as close to the "barrier" as possible. They moved perhaps twelve inches, no more. I had a bird's eye view of these manoeuvrings as I was on the top deck overlooking the aft portion of the ferry. The two cars behind them were encouraged to touch the bumpers of the cars in front. About eighteen inches had now been created, and not surprisingly made absolutely no difference to our situation. Meanwhile, the JCB attempted another mission, this time taking up a different angle. The juggernaut loaded down with scrap metal, undoubtedly the main culprit of our predicament, now had only eighteen inches to move forwards. Hardly sufficient to get us off the sandbank. There was also clearly a concern amongst the crew members and truck driver as to whether with his load he could just edge forward a little, or whether with the sheer weight he'd hit the bumpers of the second row of cars, which in turn would hit the first row, which in turn would break the thin chain and cars would end up in the river. Fortunately at this point, the JCB gave one further push with it's bucket, and we were off the sandbank. Yeah!

So the two hour crossing became four hours, sitting on the hard rusty metal deck. Ouch. With hindsight, I thought that I'd rather have crossed in the little wooden boats and been carried to shore on the shoulders of someone, risking falling in the water than enduring the four hours on this wreck of a ferry.

I was a little bemused by a couple of the kids during the journey. One of the girls, with olive coloured skin and long black African plaited hair had been holding Craig's hand when on shore. I had assumed they were boyfriend and girlfriend. However, on the ferry, the sullen girl with ivy crawling up her arms, was lying on the deck with her head in Craig's lap. All very peculiar. I just didn't understand the youngsters of today.

I was shattered by the time I got back to the hotel, and ached all over from the last uncomfortable four hours, so had a quick dinner of Barracuda fish, washed down with a couple of beers and then retired for the night to recover.

Day 6 - Chilling

This was my planned day of chilling out.

I headed down to breakfast and was about to tuck into my scrambled egg when Liz, Mr Arrogant's partner slipped into the seat opposite me.

"Have you seen Sarah's hair. Doesn't it look really lovely," she uttered in her plumy accent.

Sarah had her hair plaited yesterday after seeing mine, and this was the first time Mrs Arrogant had spoken to me. The words, not actually uttered at the end of her sentence, but I could hear them anyway were "Unlike yours which looks frightfully awful." She then asked me what I was planning for the day and I told her that it was a chill out day, though I may take a massage as my back was killing me from sitting on the deck yesterday.

"I use Anna ALL the time," she drawled. "She is amazing. Magic hands. Do mention my name if you use her and I'm sure she'll give you an extra special massage." With that she whisked herself off back to her table without another word. I still didn't really understand why she had come over to speak to me anyway.

I wanted to get a little souvenir to take home, plus I needed some more cash, so I asked reception to call a taxi to take me down to Bakhar market, stopping off at the ATM en route. They called me a green tourist taxi, and he wanted 300 Dalasi just to take me down the road and back. I knew it was Sunday, but I said to reception that it was a bit expensive and perhaps they could call me a regular yellow taxi.

"No, no. The green ones are much more reliable. We only use green taxis because if you forget something, such as leaving your shopping on the back seat, they will bring it back, you will see it again, whereas with a yellow taxi you are likely to never see it again. We only like the green taxis."

Considering that the rest of the week they'd been calling yellow taxis for me, this argument was a little weak, but I guessed that I was at least injecting some money into their economy, so I climbed into the taxi for the one-mile journey. I also suspected that the green taxi waiting by reception was a friend of the Sunday receptionist, and that he'd get a back-hander of sorts. Yes, I could have walked, but walking a two-mile round trip with pestering, flying rats and an army of Velcro's, would have taken at least an hour.

Bakhau craft market was a row of shack stalls, about a dozen in all. Apart from one that just specialised in wood carvings and another in batik materials, the others all sold exactly the same stock, namely: a range of wooden carvings consisting mainly of masks, bowls, animals and half naked African women; a range of batik material – the same range in each shop; and jewellery made of wood, stones or plastic beads, again, all the same stock. They must have all used the same distributor.

Not only did they all sell pretty much the same thing, but I had the same conversation as I moved from shop to shop. It was a bit like a speeded up scene from Groundhog Day.

"Hello! How are you?"

"Very well thank you, and you?"

"Very well. You come into my shop?" which in reality was more of an order than a question.

"I'm just browsing."

"You come in. I give you very good price."

"I have no doubt." Did I actually say that or was it just my thoughts?

"You are my first customer today, and I always give my first customer a very good price. You buy one and I give you another for free!"

Oh no! I cringed at the fact that BOGOFs had reached The Gambia...or perhaps they started in Gambia.... If I even hovered a second looking at something, they picked up on potential interest, and then the more intimate conversation started.

"Where you from?"

"England."

"England. Very nice. Where in England?"

"In the south."

"The south? Very nice. I give you a good price boss woman."

"I'm not a boss woman."

"You will look very nice in that necklace."

Although I had this conversation a dozen times as I made my way from one shack shop to the next, my eyes were quickly trained to do a dart around scan of the bric-a-brac, and then to move them on quickly when I spotted something that caught my eye, thereby avoiding the giveaway of potential interest. The only thing that seemed to distinguish between the shops was the amount of dust. Some were incredibly clean with carved wooden African breasts polished and shining like Belisha beacons. Others looked like their wares hadn't seen a duster since they were made and a couple even looked like they've been bombarded with sand storms for at least two months.

I eventually left the market with two wooden beaded necklaces and a beautiful carved pair of parrots with a fledgling. With my trophies in the car we returned to the hotel via a futile stop at the ATM. It didn't even let my card slip in, let alone get to the stage of actually giving me some cash. Bugger. I'd have to change money at Ngala at their inflated hotel rates.

Back at the lodge I requested that I would like to book Anna for a back massage. I said today or tomorrow around 4.00pm to 5.00pm would be fine.

"4.00pm today it is." the lad behind reception says.

"But you haven't checked her availability?"

"4.00pm today she will be free."

"But it's Sunday!"

"It will be fine."

"Do you not want to check it out with Anna first?"

"No. It will be fine".

I spent the rest of the day sunbathing, although it was not especially sunny. Overcast but as hot as ever and ridiculously sultry. I thought I felt a drop of rain, so retreated to my room as I wasn't tanning anyway. I just made it back to the room when the heavens opened and wow did it pour. I'd only seen sheet rain like this once before, in Brazil, where it was so strong that visibility was reduced to almost zero. This was a typical West African summer storm when it moves from a single raindrop to a flood in the blink of an eye. I made it back to the room in the nick of time, but the others on the loungers would have had to take shelter in the towel hut or be sliced to death with the shards of rain if they'd risked running back to the hotel. The rain fell solidly for about fifteen minutes and for the first time in the week it felt pleasantly cool and fresh. Breathable, un-clammy and crisp. I stood on my balcony and soaked up the freshness, however this only lasted as long as the rain did, and within fifteen minutes of the rain stopping, it was back to terminal humidity.

At this point, Anna arrived and I spent the next hour having a great therapeutic massage. Mrs Arrogant was right about one thing, Anna did indeed have magical hands, and homed in very quickly on the injured muscles and even found some I wasn't aware of until her fingers pressed in deep.

Anna also spoke pretty good English, and gave me a slice of

her family history

"I have two children, but my husband died last year." She said

"I'm sorry to hear that," I replied. Assuming he was of similar age to her, then he couldn't have been much more that fifty.

"I am not sorry," she continued, "he was not a nice man. No good at all. He couldn't keep it in his pants!" and with this she chortled loudly.

"I am a very good Catholic, so even though he was a very bad man, once I was married to him I had to stay with him, but I am not sad that now he is gone. The two children I told you about are my children, however I have brought up many children."

"Were you a nanny or child minder?" I asked. Again she chortled.

"Oh no. They were his children. Five of them. All little bastards, each to different women. They were just left with me by his mistresses, because they didn't want to have to bring up a child with no father or money." Her tone turned from being matter of fact to being soft and warm. "It wasn't their fault you know. The children. They didn't ask to be brought into the world in such circumstances. They are the innocents. I treated them the same as my own kids, and brought them up as if they were mine. They all had a private education, so that they could do something with their lives having had such an unfortunate start." Wow, that was some commitment.

"It must have cost you a lot of money to give seven children a private education." I replied.

"I was lucky. My parents knew that it was very important to have an education and a skill, and I was sent to Sweden to train in massage. I do relaxing massage, but am also trained in all sorts of sport injury massage. I am highly qualified, and for this I earned sufficient money to school the children." I had absolutely no doubt whatsoever that she was highly qualified, as my back felt the best it had for weeks. It was worth every penny spent.

After Anna had left, I felt like having a sleep because of the drowsing effect of the massage, but I wrote a little of the diary instead, read a couple of chapters and then headed down to dinner. It was Africa night so I wore my one long dress I'd taken with me, which coincidentally had an African style about it, and made more of an effort than usual with my make-up. The rest of the week the dress code had been very casual.

Richard and Sarah were sitting at the bar when I walked in and they beckoned me over and asked if I wanted to sit with them for dinner. We were planning to have a table outside, however after the afternoon rain storm, there were giant flying ants everywhere, so we swapped our table for one under cover, but with a large standing fan directed towards us as there was no breeze to cool us that evening.

We passed another excellent evening swapping stories and having a good laugh. I told them about Mr Arrogant and his run in with Peter a couple of days before and Richard said that they had been chatting with Mrs Arrogant, who seemed pleasant enough, when Mr Arrogant had approached them. He didn't say hello, and indeed didn't join in the conversation, and his body language apparently was appalling. It screamed "why are you talking to these morons – come away – lets go and eat."

Richard and Sarah also told me a great story of taking their grandchildren to Lapland to see Santa. They were about 5 and 8 years old at the time, still at the age when they could believe in Father Christmas and find the whole experience of seeing the reindeers and sledges magical. They continued to say that their daughter was really peeved not to have gone also. At various points throughout the rest of the evening we joked about Carole's revenge. For example, they had had a call earlier in the week from Carole, who had been keeping an eye on their house, to say that their freezer had broken, defrosted and there was a shed load of rotting food.

"She probably pulled the plug out because you didn't take her to see Santa," I quipped, and we all started laughing again.

I told them my tale of meeting Santa. I was working for Kraft Foods back in 1986 and we went to Helsinki for a sales conference. Usually the day after the gala dinner, sightseeing trips were arranged, however on that occasion, at the end of the gala dinner, which featured an extremely entertaining Bob Monkhouse, we were told that there was an air traffic controllers strike in the UK the next day, so we would have to be ready to leave the hotel at 6.30am the next morning. Well, did the sales guys moan or did they moan. The said it was the worst conference they had been to because they didn't get to see anything of the foreign county as they usually did, and to be up early enough to leave at 6.30am, probably with hangovers, just wasn't worth considering. So the following morning we were all standing outside of the hotel, bleary eyed, ready to go to the airport, and with the sales guys still moaning about what a crap conference it had been.

About twenty minutes into the flight the pilot announced that we were not on our way to the UK as per the flight schedule, but if we looked outside we would see a snow-capped landscape, and in twenty minutes we would be landing inside the arctic circle! I was in marketing and had only been with the company a month, so was excited just to have gone abroad for a conference and wasn't bothered that we had an early start home the next day. On arrival we were taken to meet Santa and his reindeers, not to mention the special barbecue of Kraft sausage rolls, and Santa gave us each a present wrapped in suitable seasonal paper. I forgot to mention – it was April. After a coach trip around the area and an explanation of what it was like to live in Lapland with half the year being predominantly dark and the other half almost always daylight, we were back to the airport and our real flight home. The sales guys had turned from Mr Grumpies to Mr Happies, and now this was deemed not to be the worst conference ever, but the best! Back on terra firma at Luton airport, I was the first to go through customs. The conversation went like this...

"Are you carrying anything that someone has given you to bring into the country?"

"Yes."

"Yes?" with incredulity, "what is it?"

"I don't know, I haven't opened it yet."

"You haven't opened it yet?" Double incredulity.

"No. I'm leaving it as a surprise for when I get home."

"Who gave it to you?"

"Santa."

"Santa????"

"Yes – and I think you had better believe me because there are another hundred people behind me who are also carrying gifts from Santa." The customs guys then realised that I was off the specially chartered plane that had just landed, and we all laughed. I doubt it would be as easy these days to bring an unopened parcel from Santa, in April, through an airport!

Richard and Sarah had been back to the school for lunch with the headmaster. They had thought it would be at his house, however it was held in the schoolroom. Just as you take wine and chocolates if you go to lunch or dinner in the UK, they had wanted to take something appropriate to the local culture. After making enquiries their gift was a sack of rice, and the headmaster was apparently over the moon with such a generous present. At the school, in addition to the headmaster, there were some other officials and some children, including the two children they specifically sponsored. There were more speeches, more entertainment and then they sat down for lunch, which was a lamb stew with Yassa sauce and seasonal vegetables. There was no cutlery, so they had to eat with their fingers. Sarah took one mouthful of lamb and then had to discreetly spit it out into a handkerchief. I asked her if the meat was rotten, and she said

"Meat? There was no meat, it was just a lump of fat and gristle, and just impossible to eat. Too tough to chew and too slimy to keep in your mouth."

She was thinking that at least she'd be able eat the vegetables, when one of the little girls, who not only had extremely dirty hands but who had been sitting next to Sarah picking her nose throughout the lunch preamble, thought that Sarah needed help with her dinner, so used her fingers to spoon some of the sauce over the vegetables. Sarah was unable to eat anymore, and Richard said she deserved an Oscar for her performance of pretending to eat for thirty minutes without any food passing her lips, so it was fair to say that they were both pretty hungry that evening.

Day 7 – Early Birds

The alarm went off at 4.45am to give me sufficient time to boil a couple of cups of coffee to wake me up, take a shower and prepare myself for the early morning bird watching excursion.

I was the first to be picked up this morning, spot on time, the only person from Ngala, and then we were off to the Sunset hotel to pick up Katie and Craig, two of the kids from the safari day who had also booked for early birds. We reached their hotel and neither were waiting. I sat on the minibus and waited and waited and waited. Eventually at 5.45am I asked Doodoo, who was our guide again for the day, what time their pickup was supposed to be, and he replied, 5.35am. I suggested that he may want to give them a wakeup call, but he pointed to the bus clock which showed 5.20 and said,

"Plenty of time Suzan, plenty of time." I showed him my watch, then he looked at the bus clock again, then his own watch, and realising that the bus clock was out by nearly half an hour, leapt off the bus and headed into the hotel foyer to find out where they were. He emerged with a sleepy looking Craig just a few minutes later.

Craig's eyes light up when he saw me, a familiar face, and he asked if he could sit next to me.

"Katie has an upset stomach so won't be joining us." He said.

We stopped at one further hotel to pick up another three people and then we were off to catch the early birds.

During the journey, Craig told me a little about himself. His degree was also in psychology and he'd had several jobs which had involved working with disturbed, abused and underprivileged children with behavioural problems. I found him a polite, eloquent and intelligent young man, especially when he explained his current personal circumstances, a problem partner and a tussle over his child, and the impact on his own mental well being. Considering that he was clearly suffering emotional issues, I found him well balanced and sensible.

Craig's heart was being shredded daily with the traumas back home and he hadn't wanted to come on this holiday, however, not only was it already paid for, but his sister had encouraged him to come thinking that it would do him good to be out doing something rather than brooding and playing the waiting game. He said he'd not been at all great the first week as he really felt the distance between himself and his young daughter, exacerbated by the fact that the first week was visiting school projects he was involved with back home, but the second week had been more bearable and he'd been able to relax a little, and there were even some parts that he'd enjoyed. I thought that perhaps he saw me as a mother figure which was why he could so freely pour his heart out. Most of the time he carried a serious face with his eyes giving away that he just wasn't in the moment. However when he did smile, it waved through his face, his eyes returned to this planet and he was a strikingly good looking lad. I was sure that it would all come out in the wash for him, and as I had the benefit of 25 years more experience, I knew that however painful something was at the time, things really do get better eventually. I didn't say this to him as I could see he was so deep in his own world and my encouraging words would have little impact at that moment, but

I did know deep down that he would be fine.

The bird sanctuary was gloriously tranquil. It was by the river and a park, for want of a better word, and had several open thatched buildings where you could take refreshments. There were also some manmade tiled pools in glistening azure blues and greens, and lovely garden ornaments tastefully placed amongst the trees. We took a boat trip down the river for about an hour, and then an hour back again. We saw quite a few birds, however they were either moving too fast to recognise, let alone photograph, or they were silhouetted, as dawn was approaching, so it was a little disappointing that we didn't see some of them in their glorious, daylight plumage. We floated through mangroves, where fresh oysters were clinging to the dangling roots.

There were some lovely wooden structures like tethered houseboats along a portion of the river, and they looked as if they would make very tranquil and romantic holiday homes. They already had visitors, a Goliath Heron, the largest Heron in Gambia and an Iguana that didn't even bat an eyelid as we slid past.

With the boat trip over, we breakfasted ashore in one of the thatched gazebos. I had expected a typical Gambian breakfast as part of the early birds experience, however we were served bacon, sausage and fried egg on toast. By the time it was served, I was most definitely ready for something to eat.

Following breakfast, we went for a short woodland walk and to see some more birds, however I was disappointed again that we saw so few colourful exotics. Richard and Sarah had been on a private bird watch tour the day before, and having seen their photos on their iPads the previous evening, they'd definitely seen more birds on an unofficial trip out than I had in the bird sanctuary. Also, I hadn't seen the elusive White Egret.

We then headed back to the hotel and I was definitely ready for lunch, so indulged in some grilled prawn with garlic butter, chips and salad. Delicious. I also had a couple of beers, which I wouldn't usually have at lunchtime, then found myself a sun longer to give both sides of my body an hour's toasting. When I stood up to return to my room, I was staggering and feel dizzy and guessed that I was a little dehydrated and possibly had mild sunstroke. I drank lots of water and lay down for an hour, arising to feel fully refreshed.

It was the last dinner that evening, and although I didn't sit with Richard and Sarah, they were on the table next to me. The food had been excellent all week, with one exception, the vegetables. There was nothing actually nothing wrong with them but with each meal we were served the exact same combination, al dente carrots, creamed spinach and a slice of courgette with mashed carrot on top. I finished eating and discretely withdrew so that Richard and Sarah could enjoy their last dinner of the holiday together.

Day 8 – Time to go home

I was up, showered and packed by 7.00am. I wanted to make the most of the last morning of sunshine and not waste time packing. My lovely parrot carving was gently cocooned amongst underwear and dirty clothes as I didn't want to risk them being snapped off their perch during the flight home. It was the last breakfast and the staff had chalked up a board for those of us leaving, saying that they loved us, would miss us and wished us a safe journey home. Okay, so it was a little cheesy, and possibly intended as a reminder for those tips envelopes we'd been told about at the beginning of the week, but it was also quite sweet. After breakfast I found a chair in the garden and did some reading before lunch. Perhaps it was because of the rain, but there were many more lizards around, so most of my time was spent finding different coloured ones and photographing them.

I had an early lunch, not because I was especially hungry, but because I knew that my next meal on board the aircraft was not for another seven or eight hours. I always eat when I have the opportunity and believe it to be because I was very impressionable when I first saw the movie, Gone With The Wind. Just before the interval, we see Scarlett o'Hara returning to Tara, starving hungry and she falls to her knees, pulls up a carrot and gnaws at it before being sick. She then shakes her fist up to the sky and says' "As God is my witness, I will never go hungry again." So I eat when I can because I don't know when the next meal will be. This may sound a little silly, as most of time you can control when you have your meals, however, when doing an international job for ICI and flying all over the world, I literally didn't know when I'd get my next meal, and if I go without regular food, I can get a severe case of the wobblies. Of course sometimes I'd be caught out. I'd eat on the plane, land, be met by a limo and then whisked off to a restaurant to meet my colleagues for dinner. Then there were other times when I'd remember being taken off to a restaurant as soon as I disembarked, so hadn't eaten on the plane, only to march straight into a business meeting with nothing more than a few shortbread biscuits on offer. So, better to be safe than wobbly, so I had the delicious garlic prawns again and fleetingly felt sorry for whoever would have to sit next to me on the flight home.

12.30, and those going home mustered in the reception hut. Mr and Mrs Arrogant were missing and a young couple said they were in the office arguing over his bill and had already been in there for an hour. Apparently Mr Arrogant had a notepad of everything eaten and drunk during the week and was meticulously checking and ticking off every item, line by line, on his bill. Not entirely surprising, but the bill added up perfectly. However, when he came to pay by card, the hotel changed the Dalasi into dollars and he was complaining and arguing that he disagreed with the extortionate exchange rate they were charging, to the extent that it could cost him between £10 and £15 extra for his holiday. They offered him the opportunity to pay cash in Dalasi, however he didn't have sufficient notes on him and the hotel exchange rate for sterling to Dalasi wasn't great either. Just before the coach arrived to take us to the airport, his flabby body wobbled out of the office, the look on his face saying that another minute and he would explode right in front of us.

We piled into the coach and were off to Banjul airport.

En route I saw a whole flock of white Egrets and chuckled to myself. The first time I was in Gambia all those years ago, I went on a boat trip which had specific ornithological interest, though at the time I had little interest in birds. There were several old dears with binoculars around their neck searching eagerly for a White Egret. Once one was spotted they screamed "oh look! A White Egret!" and they would all grab their binoculars and look in the same direction, enjoying their group orgasm. Two minutes later another White Egret, then another, and indeed a consistent appearance of Egrets throughout the boat trip. My husband at the time and I looked at each other with a glance of despair, each non verbally sating "not another bloody White Egret!". Yet, here I was twentyish years later, with an interest in birds, and throughout the week I hadn't seen one White Egret until now on the coach journey back to the airport where I saw a whole flock. I smiled to myself knowing how things have changed over the years.

We arrived at the airport and piled off the coach and into the departure hall. Mr Arrogant literally elbowed his way off the coach, and through the crowd to take up pole position in the queue. It was of course a total waste of time as the seats had already been allocated, but I could now see into his head and he wanted to build in contingency time should he not get the seats he wanted. Mrs Arrogant meanwhile had left her newly purchased hat back at Ngala reception. Babou J told her to jump in a taxi as she had plenty of time before check-in closed.

However, she was loudly claiming that it wasn't her fault that she forgot her hat, so she'd be damned if she was going to pay for a taxi, and insisted that the coach took her back. Yes, extremely flawed logic, but the coach did indeed take her back to the Lodge. Mr Arrogant remained firmly at the front of the queue without offering to step in and help.

Getting through the airport and past officialdom was relatively easy, certainly a lot easier getting out of the country than getting in. I settled down in the first class lounge for which I'd paid a fifteen pounds access fee, however it was air conditioned and quiet, so worth every penny. I saw Mr Arrogant settle outside catching the last few rays of sun, which would only make his round red podgy face even more red. En route to the lounge I saw Mrs Arrogant with hat in hand looking around. I pointed to the terrace and said "your other half is out there." She glared at me and then replied,

"He is NOT my other half," and stormed off. I never did work out what their relationship was. They shared a room, dined together and sunbathed together yet treated each other as strangers and not even friends.

The flight home was significantly less hassle than the one out and I reclined my seat, closed my eyes and slept.

To find out more about the author, visit:

www.susanrogersauthor.co.uk